Pro CSS3 Layout Techniques

Sam Hampton-Smith

Apress®

Pro CSS3 Layout Techniques

Sam Hampton-Smith
Elgin, Morayshire, United Kingdom

ISBN-13 (pbk): 978-1-4302-6502-3   ISBN-13 (electronic): 978-1-4302-6503-0
DOI 10.1007/978-1-4302-6503-0

Library of Congress Control Number: 2016938679

Managing Director: Welmoed Spahr
Acquisitions Editor: Ben Renow-Clarke
Developmental Editor: Matthew Moodie
Technical Reviewer: Jeffrey Sambells
Editorial Board: Steve Anglin, Pramila Balen, Louise Corrigan, James DeWolf, Jonathan Gennick, Robert Hutchinson, Celestin Suresh John, Michelle Lowman, James Markham, Susan McDermott, Matthew Moodie, Jeffrey Pepper, Douglas Pundick, Ben Renow-Clarke, Gwenan Spearing
Coordinating Editor: Rita Fernando
Copy Editor: Tiffany Taylor
Compositor: SPi Global
Indexer: SPi Global

Distributed to the book trade worldwide by Springer Science+Business Media New York, 233 Spring Street, 6th Floor, New York, NY 10013. Phone 1-800-SPRINGER, fax (201) 348-4505, e-mail orders-ny@springer-sbm.com, or visit www.springer.com. Apress Media, LLC is a California LLC and the sole member (owner) is Springer Science + Business Media Finance Inc (SSBM Finance Inc). SSBM Finance Inc is a Delaware corporation.

For information on translations, please e-mail rights@apress.com, or visit www.apress.com.

Apress and friends of ED books may be purchased in bulk for academic, corporate, or promotional use. eBook versions and licenses are also available for most titles. For more information, reference our Special Bulk Sales–eBook Licensing web page at www.apress.com/bulk-sales.

Any source code or other supplementary materials referenced by the author in this text is available to readers at www.apress.com. For detailed information about how to locate your book's source code, go to www.apress.com/source-code/.

Printed on acid-free paper

To my wonderful kids. Remember to strive!

Contents at a Glance

Contents

About the Author

Sam Hampton-Smith has worked with the Web since the mid 1990s and was an early adopter and proponent for CSS, the semantic Web, and separation of style and substance. He writes regularly for web and graphic design magazines, has contributed to numerous books, and previously was a visiting lecturer in multimedia design at the University of the Highlands and Islands. Sam loves making music, photography, being a little geeky, and exploring the world. He lives in Scotland with his four children.

About the Technical Reviewer

Jeffrey Sambells is a graphic designer and self-taught web applications developer best known for his unique ability to merge the visual world of graphics with the mental realm of code. With a bachelor of technology degree in graphic communications management along with a minor in multimedia, Jeffrey was originally trained for the traditional paper-and-ink printing industry, but he soon realized the world of pixels and code was where his ideas would prosper. In late 1999, he cofounded We-Create, Inc., an Internet software company based in Waterloo, Ontario, which began many long nights of challenging and creative innovation. Currently, as director of research and development for We-Create, Jeffrey is responsible for investigating new and emerging Internet technologies and integrating them using web standards-compliant methods. In late 2005, he also became a Zend Certified Engineer. When not playing at the office, Jeffrey enjoys a variety of hobbies from photography to woodworking. When the opportunity arises, he also enjoys floating in a canoe on the lakes of Algonquin Provincial Park or going on an adventurous, map-free, drive with his wife. Jeffrey also maintains a personal web site at JeffreySambells.com, where he shares thoughts, ideas, and opinions about web technologies, photography, design, and more. He lives in Ontario, Canada, with his wife, Stephanie, his daughter, Addison, and their little dog, Milo.

Acknowledgments

This book would never have seen the light of day had it not been for the enormous amount of support I received from my family. Beatrice, Bethan, Dylan, Finnian, Eliot, Jasper, Linda, and Lorna have all in their own way provided me with the motivation, belief, and determination to succeed.

I am indebted to the wonderful people at Apress, without whom you wouldn't be holding a shiny book in your hands. It's been an emotional and difficult journey at times, and it hasn't always been rosy and evergreen, but we made it! I couldn't have gotten here without Louise Corrigan, who originally brought me to Apress, and Ben Renow-Clarke, who was my guide throughout the process. Both showed enormous amounts of patience and belief in me. Kevin Shea, Tom Welsh, and Jeffrey Pepper all helped me to hone and refine my writing and gave me helpful pointers along the way. Christine Ricketts and Rita Fernando both provided excellent reviews and edits. And to the small army of people who just get on with the job of making an author's musings look, read, and feel like a book: I thank you all from the bottom of my heart.

Finally, thanks to my many friends who have offered me encouragement, kind words, and sage counsel. You've each helped me to overcome obstacles, challenges, and an author's natural self-doubt. I am an extremely lucky man, and I shall be forever grateful.

Introduction

In the mid 1990s, I was working for a bank when I heard about a new, exciting, emerging technology: the World Wide Web. Feeling a sense of great anticipation, I spent my entire month's salary on a PC so I could experience it for myself. My partner had a small explosion at my profligacy, but I had a real sense at the time that the Web was going to blossom into perhaps the most exciting, creative medium we had yet seen. I wanted to be riding that wave!

A matter of a few short years later, I was working full-time as a web designer and developer, and the trend was already starting to move away from table-based design layout toward a new, emerging technology: CSS. I can remember espousing the benefits of this innovation to my colleagues at the time and feeling genuinely excited for the future of design on the Web. Of course, the earliest versions of CSS were more about transferring stylistic control from HTML to a separate document, but the seeds of possibility were sown and captured my imagination.

I hope you will enjoy a similar journey while reading this book. CSS has come a long way since those early days. Yet I continue to be amazed and inspired on an almost daily basis by what can be achieved using this simple, text-based, human-readable language. Web design remains an exciting field to work in, and the possibilities keep expanding! I can't wait to see what you create with the CSS3 layout techniques you'll find in this book.

If you have any suggestions or corrections, I'd love to hear from you. In the meantime, turn the page, and let's get started:

1. Overcoming the Layout Challenges of the Web

2. Layout Modules in CSS: the Old and the New

3. Where We've Been: Position, Float, and Display

4. CSS Multi-column Layout

5. CSS Flexible Box Layout

6. CSS Grid Layout

7. CSS Regions Layout

8. Supporting Older Browsers

9. Speeding Up Workflow: CSS Libraries and Frameworks

10. What the Future Holds for CSS Layout

CHAPTER 1

■ ■ ■

Overcoming the Layout Challenges of the Web

Welcome to *Pro CSS3 Layout Techniques*!

Although it would be unfair to say that style is more important than substance, it's certainly true that we all expect web sites to look good, to react responsively to our devices, and to rival other media for engagement. This means that as web designers, we've got the weight of expectation on us to generate ever-more-intuitive layouts, user-friendly presentations, and device-agnostic code. Although we're up for the challenge, some of the core tools we have at our disposal either were never intended for layout or are now over a decade old. The Web has moved on, but layout tools haven't—until the arrival and implementation of CSS3, that is.

This book will cover the following topics:

- Taking advantage of CSS3 layout modules

- Determining what's viable today

- Discovering what will be available for use in a live environment soon

- Learning the best-practice approaches to layout using the CSS Level 2.1 specification where CSS3 is not available

Before we all get too excited about the new toys, it's well worth understanding why we find ourselves in this position in the first place. And in order to get a proper grasp, we need to look back at the development of both HTML (Hypertext Markup Language) and CSS (Cascading Style Sheets). Don't worry: this review isn't going to be an exhaustive trip down memory lane, but it will serve you well when you're next using CSS to craft a layout.

HTML Attributes and Tags

When the Web was in its very early days, HTML was used both for markup and for styling. HTML attributes and tags defined the way a page looked. Decisions about how to mark up content were as likely to stem from a tag's default visual characteristics as from any sense of semantic hierarchy. Consider the following examples and their uses:

- `<h1>` tags for big, bold text, but also to signify the most important piece of information on the page.

- `<p>` for small text, but also to show paragraph text that provided the meat on the bones of the headings.

Electronic supplementary material The online version of this chapter (doi:10.1007/978-1-4302-6503-0_1) contains supplementary material, which is available to authorized users.

- `<center>` tags to align paragraphs and tables. Originally they were intended as a way to present tabular data only. These tags came to be used for creating sophisticated mult-column layouts that simply wouldn't have been possible with the limited set of tags and formatting attributes available within the language.

Although this approach was incredibly resourceful and creative, it led to some dreadful code that was both difficult to read and awkward to maintain. As layout demands became more complex, so tables came to be nested within each other—often several layers deep. Visually redundant transparent spacer GIFs were increasingly used to ensure the correct positioning of elements. It became common for a simple page to contain hundreds or thousands of lines of unintelligible code like that shown in Listing 1-1.

Listing 1-1. Example of a Vast Listing to Create a Basic Two-Column Layout

```
<FONT FACE=TIMES COLOR=#FF0000 SIZE=3>
 <H2><I>WELCOME TO MY WEBSITE</I></H2>
  <CENTER>
    <TABLE WIDTH=720 HEIGHT=480 BORDER=2 BGCOLOR=BLACK>
     <TR>
       <TD BACKGROUND=texture.gif>
         <TABLE WIDTH=360 HEIGHT=480 BORDER=0>
           <TR>
             <TD>
                 <IMG SRC=spacer.gif WIDTH=360 HEIGHT=10><BR>
                 <H1>ABOUT MY SITE</H1>
                 <P>...</P>
             </TD>
           </TR>
          </TABLE>
       </TD>
       <TD BACKGROUND=texture2.gif>
        <TABLE WIDTH=360 HEIGHT=480 BORDER=0>
          <TR>
            <TD>
                <IMG SRC=spacer.gif WIDTH=360 HEIGHT=10><BR>
                <H1>ABOUT ME</H1>
                <P>...</P>
            </TD>
          </TR>
         </TABLE>
       </TD>
     </TR>
    </TABLE>
  </CENTER>
</FONT>
```

This approach to coding and maintaining web sites raised issues that were obvious to everybody working with HTML. The Web needed a way to separate content from style, so the World Wide Web Consortium (W3C) stepped up to the task, developing the CSS Level 1 specification.

The Arrival of CSS

As the Web started to move beyond a simple text-based medium and became a more visual, magazine-style experience, it quickly became apparent that the limitations imposed by HTML styling were going to be an issue. The W3C, charged with defining standards for the Web, determined that it would be more sensible to separate style from content, and started work on a new language that would control the aesthetic treatment of content separate from the semantic meaning of that content. The solution was Cascading Style Sheets (CSS), the basis of all design and layout on the modern web page.

CSS Level 1

CSS Level 1 (CSS1) wasn't intended to act as a solution for implementing layout. Instead, the idea was to replace all the basic visual characteristics, such as color, font, margin, and border, that had been specified using HTML tags and attributes. The result was the following limited set of properties:

- Width and height of block-level elements

- Float, and clear of floating elements

- Margins and padding

- Background colors and images

- Borders

- Fonts and font styles

- List styles

- Some basic alignment

CSS1 allowed designs to take the basic styling of individual elements outside the HTML code itself. For the first time, the way a web site looked could be controlled from a single external file. This had massive benefits for the maintenance and consistency of page designs, because a single line of CSS code could now affect an entire web site. Previously, a simple heading color change meant editing every single page within a web site individually.

It took web browsers some time to adopt the new CSS specification because of a lack of competition in the browser market and relatively slow demand from designers. It wasn't until the late 1990s that designers could rely on the commonly used browsers, such as Netscape Navigator and Microsoft Internet Explorer, to parse and render CSS code with anything close to accuracy. Coincidentally, Microsoft and Netscape were battling for supremacy. Internet Explorer, shown in Figure 1-1, was the eventual victor.

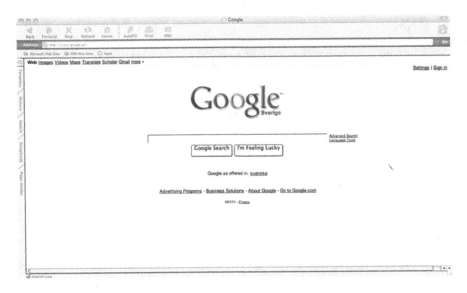

Figure 1-1. *Internet Explorer on the Mac was the first CSS-compliant browser*

Perhaps you are familiar with the use of floating elements as a system for creating layouts. However, the `float` and `clear` properties introduced with CSS1 were never intended for this purpose. They were meant to provide a CSS facsimile of the `ALIGN=LEFT` and `ALIGN=RIGHT` properties that had previously been part of HTML. The plan was to use them on images, allowing text to flow around elements automatically. Chapter 2 discusses how to use floating elements effectively.

You may have noticed properties for width and height in the specification, which could be used to define the dimensions of elements. But their purpose was simply to replicate the same properties that were previously used in HTML as attributes on images, tables, and other block-level elements.

CSS1 was clearly a landmark for the Web. As it was implemented by browsers in the late 1990s, the W3C started work on the next iteration of the cascading stylesheet language: CSS Level 2.

CSS Level 2

One purpose of the design of CSS Level 2 was to implement some layout control in the stylesheet. This first attempt at moving layout from HTML to CSS was based on the table model that web designers had become accustomed to. A key new property introduced was `display`, and part of the specification provided for a value of `table-cell` to be applied. (See Figure 1-2.) This value, when properly rendered, lets you create a layout like that achieved using a table, complete with equal-height columns.

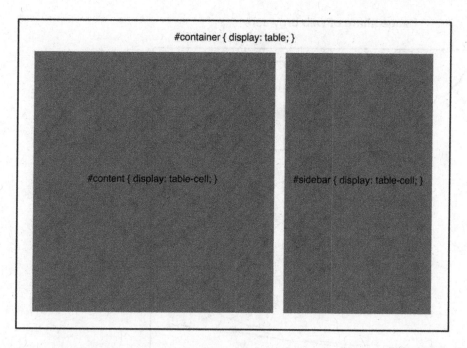

Figure 1-2. *CSS2 introduced the* `display: table-cell` *property to mimic the existing tabular layout solution being used by designers*

Sadly, not every browser supported the CSS2 standard, so it was effectively unusable on the Web. Although many browsers supported `display: table-cell`, Internet Explorer 6 did not. Consequently, reliable layout remained firmly in the realm of HTML tables. Furthermore, browser vendors interpreted the loosely written CSS2 specification in slightly different ways. Therefore, browsers rendered the same page inconsistently, frustrating both designers and consumers.

The W3C had already started working on the next version of CSS—level 3. However, recognizing the deficiencies in the CSS2 specification, the group shelved CSS3 and instead spent a long time working on addressing the interoperability problems arising from CSS2, eventually developing a successor in the form of CSS Level 2.1.

Because Internet Explorer enjoyed a practical monopoly, the majority of web sites were designed with its approach to rendering in mind. Eventually, designers adopted the separation of style and content, but they were forced to use floats and absolute positioning to craft layouts. As you've already seen, these properties were never intended as tools for layout. But the ever-resourceful web design community found ways to hijack them and generate clever layouts without the use of tables.

Browsers

Figure 1-3 shows the balance of power shifting toward Google's Chrome browser. However, a large proportion of users rely on Internet Explorer.

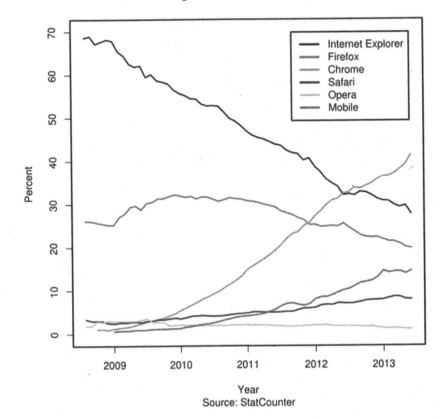

Figure 1-3. *Market share statistics from 2013 show browser usage. Image from StatCounter.com*

Let's take a look at the following examples:

- Firefox
- Internet Explorer
- Chrome

Firefox

After America Online (AOL) bought the Netscape browser in 1999, the source code was *open sourced*, allowing the developer community to contribute toward it. This admirable action led to the formation of an entirely new approach to browser functionality. The result was the Mozilla Foundation and the arrival in 2004 of a new web browser: Firefox.

Firefox single-handedly kick-started a new browser war. Microsoft remained the dominant browser, with a market share in the region of 90%, but Firefox slowly chipped away at its dominance. This eventually forced Microsoft to update the aging Internet Explorer after a six-year hiatus.

Internet Explorer

Internet Explorer 7 was released in 2007. It brought tabbed browsing to users, but very little in the way of standards adoption or additional support for CSS to designers.

Support for `display: table-cell` was introduced with Internet Explorer 8 in the late 2000s, and with it a degree of interoperability was ultimately achieved. Frustratingly, there remained the problem of Internet Explorer 6 being used by more than half the Web's users.

■ **Note**   Even today, Internet Explorer 6 has around 1% market share. Most web designers are now choosing to ignore this segment of the market, because the time it takes to provide support is disproportionate to the diminishing benefit returned.

Chrome

While Microsoft continued to drag its feet, Firefox gained popularity, and a new contender was introduced to the market. Search-engine giant Google developed its own branded browser based on the open-source WebKit project and released it at the very end of 2008. Chrome (see Figure 1-4) soon overtook Firefox as the Web's second-most popular browser, and it took great strides toward achieving full CSS2.1 compliance.

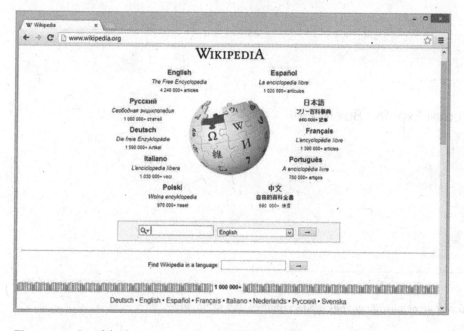

Figure 1-4. *Google's Chrome is now the world's most widely used browser*

The CSS Box Model

In the period between 2000 and 2009, web designers had to contend with the very real headache of vastly different rendering engines displaying their code in completely distinct manners. The single biggest issue was the *CSS box-model* (see Figure 1-5), which was used to determine the width of elements from the combination of specified width, height, margin, and padding. Thanks to the loosely written CSS2 specification, the box model was interpreted differently by Microsoft than the rest of the browser vendor community, leading to inconsistent rendering of documents between competing browsers; pages failed to render as expected in browsers other than Internet Explorer 6. As a result, workarounds, shivs, and hacks were employed to create layouts that were based in CSS2.1 specification-compliant code but were adapted to also work in the non-compliant IE6 rendering engine.

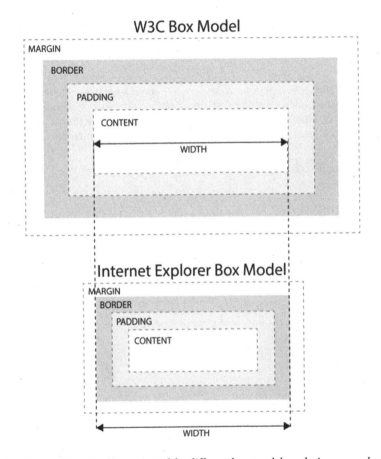

Figure 1-5. An illustration of the different box-model rendering across browsers

Microsoft is currently inviting users to ditch Internet Explorer 6 and consider it nothing more than a bad memory. However, a large proportion of the browser market share still uses the Internet Explorer 6 rendering approach thanks to Internet Explorer 7 and 8's compatibility mode. Consequently, it's common to see specialist stylesheets aimed at Microsoft's browsers. Furthermore, entire JavaScript libraries are included in a page simply to polyfill compliant rendering of layout.

In response to the difficulties in achieving interoperability between different browsers, a series of tests was developed to help measure different browsers' performance against the CSS specifications. These ACID tests were used by standards proponents to pressure browser vendors, including Microsoft, into improving their software.

Finally, in the mid-to-late 2000s, Microsoft started the process of developing standards-compliant versions of Internet Explorer: IE8 arrived in 2008, and IE9 followed in 2011. At the same time, a revolution was taking place in the mobile sector with the release of devices such as the iPhone. These new Internet-capable smartphones supported the elements of the freshly developed CSS3 specification, alongside HTML5, and added further pressure on the incumbent market leader to adopt standards.

CSS Level 3

CSS Level 3 is different than the previous iterations in that it's *modular*. This allows the CSS Working Group to release different parts of the specification as they mature, and browser vendors are able to adopt functionality rapidly. The CSS Level 3 modular approach is broadly split into four elements:

- Selectors and logic

- Decorative effects

- Typography (including support for internationalization)

- Layout

Most interestingly, the layout aspect encapsulates a series of new modules that offer flexibility and standardization in page layout that has never before been seen on the Web. Frustratingly, even with this new specification, we're continuing to struggle under the shadow of old browsers and incomplete implementations.

CSS Layout Modules

CSS Level 3 adds a range of new layout tools to the designer's arsenal. Each of these modules provides an exciting approach to crafting layouts using only CSS. The modules will change the way you author your styles and, crucially, your HTML markup.

Rather than a single approach to crafting layout, four principal modules are in development. Each includes its own concepts, rules, and, most important, browser support. The following chapters look in depth at each of these modules:

- CSS Multi-column Layout module

- CSS Flexible Box Layout (Flexbox) module

- CSS Grid Layout module

- CSS Regions Layout module

You get a proper overview of each module in Chapter 2, before Chapters 4–7 dive into full detail in a dedicated chapter per module. In the meantime, you can whet your appetite by taking a quick look at what each module can achieve layout-wise.

CSS Multi-Column Layout

CSS Multi-column Layout is the easiest of the new layout modules to grasp and implement. It's also the module with the most mature browser support, although it's potentially the least useful of the modules for advanced layouts.

The multi-column layout (see Figure 1-6) does exactly what you might expect: it makes it easy to flow content automatically into multiple columns, which can adapt to the available space so that smaller screens render fewer columns than larger screens. Chapter 4 examines this module.

Figure 1-6. *CSS Multi-column Layout rendering content into a column-based layout*

CSS Flexible Box Layout

CSS Flexible Box Layout (or Flexbox) has been through several different revisions. Thanks to some early browser implementations, there are many now-defunct examples on the Web. This has led to confusion in the web design community; but now that the specification has stabilized, there's reasonably good cross-browser support for the module.

Flexbox isn't designed to provide a complete layout solution for web sites, but it does let you create elements such as toolbars and tabbed areas that respond to the device being used to view them (see Figure 1-7). Chapter 5 looks in depth at the Flexbox module.

Figure 1-7. *Flexbox helps solve some common user interface design problems*

CSS Grid Layout

CSS Grid Layout is one of the most exciting layout modules because it allows design to be truly separated from presentation for the first time. Elements can be reordered using CSS Grid Layout, so it doesn't matter to the layout in which order the markup arrives. This is fantastic news for designers striving to create meaningful, semantic markup, not to mention that the module allows layout control within a defined grid complete with vertical alignment (see Figure 1-8). Chapter 6 examines all the details and browser support.

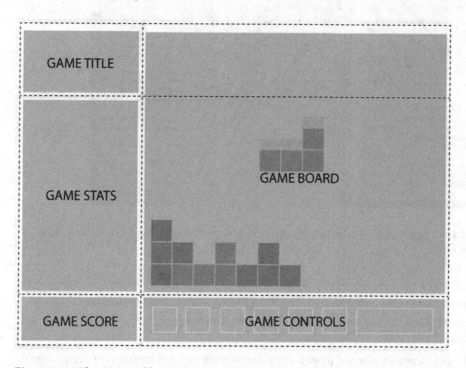

Figure 1-8. *The CSS Grid layout brings a flexible and reliable grid layout option to the Web for perhaps the first time*

CSS Regions Layout

CSS Regions Layout allow for the complex flow of content from one area to another in a magazine-style layout. This kind of sophistication in layout is beyond the other layout modules. It can be used to create dynamic, fluid layouts that are responsive to different devices (see Figure 1-9). CSS Regions Layout is not yet a fully mature module, but Chapter 7 examines all the details, including current browser support.

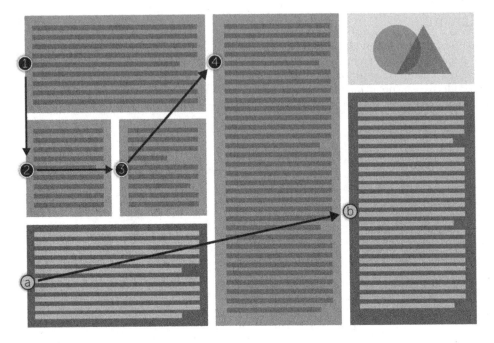

Figure 1-9. *CSS Regions Layout offers an exciting way to position content in and around elements without affecting document flow*

___

■ **Note** There are also some emerging layout modules that, although not yet part of the CSS specification, offer even more layout options. You see some of these toward the end of this book.

___

As you might expect, there are a host of potential problems with using CSS3 modules currently: some are still in development, whereas others are fairly mature. Some browsers have almost fully implemented the individual modules' standards, but others continue to work toward incorporating or in some cases defining them. It can be a minefield, but this book guides you safely through the pitfalls!

How This Book Will Help You

Now that you know what you're up against, let's quickly look at what you can expect to get out of reading this book. It's my intention to help you understand the key CSS layout techniques you can employ in your web site design approach.

CSS3 offers a huge range of exciting possibilities, and this book looks at each of the key layout modules. A word of warning: you'll change the way you construct web site layouts as a consequence of reading this book! But with that said, you'll also see some of the limitations—with the standards themselves or, as often as not, imposed by the browser software that people are using to access the Web.

By the end of this book, you'll have a realistic view of what you can do today, as well as a good idea of what will be possible in the next year or two. You'll also see a series of useful examples of polyfill techniques that can provide a graceful fallback for your layouts.

Of course, no CSS layout book would be useful if it ignored the large percentage of users on the Web who continue to use older browser software. So, you'll also see the latest best-practice approach to layout using only CSS2.1, learning the concepts along the way. Although I assume you're familiar with CSS2.1, the next chapter starts with this topic.

Summary

CSS3 is still emerging, but much of it can be safely used today. Layout modules such as Flexbox offer a reliable solution to some very real challenges faced by web designers. CSS has come a long way since the early days of the Web, and the past few years have seen a huge acceleration in the development of the language. This book will give you a quick grasp of the core principles behind each of the main layout modules in development and show you how to use the modules in the real world. Let's get started!

CHAPTER 2

■ ■ ■

Layout Modules in CSS: the Old and the New

This chapter will help you get a firm footing in the core layout concepts associated with CSS. If you're familiar with CSS2.1, you know much of this inside out already, but there may be some concepts you didn't realize CSS supported (because browser support has been so poor historically).

The chapter takes a quick tour of all the different layout paradigms that CSS offers, starting with the original version of CSS: level 1. Note that each of the layout solutions offered by CSS has been implemented as a module. Until CSS3, the entire CSS specification for each level was contained in an all-encompassing module, whereas each is now split into its own separate module; but for simplicity, I talk about each approach as if it were a separate module.

As I mentioned in the first chapter, pre-CSS there wasn't much in the way of layout control offered by HTML. Designers found an ingenious method to craft sophisticated layouts: hacking the HTML specification by using tables to position elements precisely on the page. Tables were a very useful layout tool because they offered a controllable solution to the positioning of individual pieces of content. HTML tables, however, were never intended to be used for layout; so, semantically speaking, the hack was a disaster. Because the entire approach was a workaround, there were also issues of maintainability and readability of content. It wasn't uncommon to find nested tables six or seven levels deep.

With the arrival of CSS1, the focus started to shift away from rendering everything—meaning both content and presentation—using HTML. Instead, the idea of separating content from the aesthetic presentation was established.

■ **Note**   This chapter talks about the different CSS levels: 1, 2, and 3. It's important to note that you don't choose which level to use when designing a web site; browsers support different levels, and each level builds on top of or alongside the existing levels. Although this book is about CSS3, the results seen on screen depend on the browser you are using—or, more important, the browser the person viewing your web site is using.

Layout Concepts

Before the introduction of CSS3, four (official) different layout modes were available via CSS. As already established, HTML alone doesn't include any layout-specific capability beyond the default behaviors applied by the user agent. It's been a journey of discovery for web designers, starting with layouts based on

© Sam Hampton-Smith 2016
S. Hampton-Smith, *Pro CSS3 Layout Techniques*, DOI 10.1007/978-1-4302-6503-0_2

tables as a method for implementing fine control over positioning, moving through the adoption of CSS in the first years of this century, and finally arriving at a degree of maturity today where issues of presentation and usability are inherently connected.

So what is CSS? Well, as designers attempted to create a more visual Web, the limitations of the HTML language quickly became apparent. As a primarily text-based system, HTML is a great way to communicate information, but it isn't a very good tool for making that information beautiful. Various attempts were made by the body responsible for the development of the HTML language to address basic styling needs, but fundamentally the original purpose of HTML was being eroded. Cascading Style Sheets (CSS) was introduced as a first step toward enabling a visual Web. Once established, CSS was rapidly adopted and iterated until it reached version 2.1 in the early 2000s, when it ground to a halt, caught up in the mire of politics and slow-moving browser development. Despite this, designers continued to experiment with what was possible with CSS as it stood, promoting it as a tool through the likes of CSS Zen Garden, which you can see in Figure 2-1.

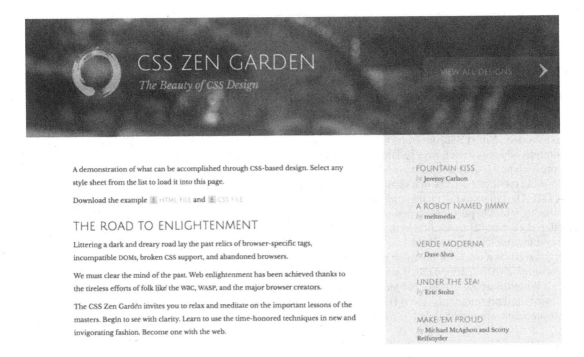

Figure 2-1. *CSS Zen Garden spearheaded the CSS revolution in the early years of the 21st century*

The Web has moved on, but the tools at our disposal haven't—until the arrival and implementation of CSS3, that is! CSS handles the appearance and styling of HTML documents, including the presentational aspects of the following:

- *Text,* including typeface selection, font size, weight, spacing, direction, and decoration

- *Colors* and *backgrounds* of different elements, including images and gradients

- *Borders* and *border effects,* including line style, size, and curved corners, and special effects such as drop shadows

- *Positioning* of different elements on the page, either within a document flow or outside the document flow

- *Margins* and *padding* of different elements on the page

- *Distribution* and *alignment* of content across different structural elements, including *columns* and *regions*

- *Transitions* and *animations*, including user-interaction control

- *Transformations* in 2D and 3D space

It's worth quickly highlighting that the latest version of CSS is still in a state of flux. Whereas with the previous version (CSS2.1), the entire specification was contained in a single module, with CSS3 the individual components have been modularized. This means the CSS Working Group (CSSWG) can iterate individual modules more quickly and efficiently, and browser vendors can implement standards without having to wait for every individual module to reach recommendation status. The downside is that the specification is split across many different modules and projects. This can make it tricky to keep track of which browser supports a specific feature and what the latest developments are in a global sense.

Since the W3C announced the development of CSS3 in 2005, the web design community has watched with a mixture of excitement and anticipation, waiting for browsers to implement the standards and open up a range of new possibilities for designs. It's been nearly a decade since CSS3 development began, but only in the past year or two has there been universal CSS2.1 support!

Despite this, CSS3 is making huge waves in the web design world, as browser vendors rapidly implement support for the new features. All the major browsers already support a sizable range of new CSS3 properties, innovative CSS3 approaches to layout, CSS-based animation, and special visual effects. It's even possible to render a 3D scene directly inside some browsers today, without the need for plug-ins or special reader software.

The Web has been historically slow to adopt new technologies, because web users needed to proactively update their browser software before those technologies were supported. Naturally, users have more interesting things to do than update their software, and as a result entire generations of users (and computers) are stuck with the original browser installed when purchased. With newer generations of laptops and desktop computers, not to mention the widespread adoption of smartphones based on the Android and iOS operating systems, browser software has also developed, and now many popular browsers automatically update themselves when a new version is available.

Until a couple of years ago, it wasn't possible to render a drop shadow on a web page without resorting to Photoshop, Adobe Flash, or some pretty complex JavaScript. And now? CSS3 makes rendering a drop shadow as simple as setting one property! Even better, thanks to the widespread adoption of this CSS3 property in today's browsers, it's a perfectly safe way to render the effect.

The CSS3 specification provides a powerful new set of tools that go far beyond simply rendering drop shadows. This book is concerned with layout options, but don't forget that CSS3 offers much more than layout control; CSS3 takes styling your web pages and apps to an entirely new level, far surpassing past possibilities. It's not a perfect tool, of course; in this chapter looks at what CSS3 isn't designed to address as well as the things it excels at.

Different Types of Layout

One of the key things to understand about modern web development is that the structure of content is independent of the presentation. CSS is specifically designed to let you define visual or auditory presentations without the need to structure HTML in a particular way, at least for the purposes of how a page is displayed to a user.

That's not to say the two things aren't explicitly linked to each other! CSS relies on a definite structure in the HTML it's applied to; but, increasingly, the layout of a page isn't dictated by the order or specific markup of content in the HTML.

This is hugely beneficial, because it allows for easier repurposing of content at a later stage, either to a new platform or as part of a design refinement. It also means you can present exactly the same content in a different way according to the profile of the device or user accessing it. This is *responsive design* (the process of engineering content to render appropriately across different devices) in practice. Another benefit is that content can be structured and delivered in a semantic order, rather than being tied to the visual design of the site.

As the CSS language has developed, the available layout options have also evolved. Each new level of CSS builds on top of the previous levels, adding functionality and capabilities. As a result, there are many potential ways to style a page with a seemingly identical layout, but each approach has different behaviors and characteristics. Let's have a quick look at what CSS offered up until the introduction of the new CSS layout modules that form part of the CSS3 specification.

Layout in CSS1

When the Web was in its very early days, HTML was used both for markup and for styling. HTML attributes and tags defined the way a page looked. Decisions about how to mark up content were as likely to stem from a tag's default visual characteristics as from any sense of semantic hierarchy. <h1> tags were used where big, bold text was needed, <p> for small text, <center> tags to align paragraphs, and tables—intended as a way to present tabular data only—to create sophisticated multi-column layouts that wouldn't have been possible with the limited set of tags and formatting attributes available in the language.

Although this approach was incredibly resourceful and creative, it led to some dreadful code that was both difficult to read and incredibly awkward to maintain. As layout demands became more complex, so tables came to be nested within each other—often several layers deep. Visually redundant transparent spacer GIFs were increasingly used to ensure the correct positioning of elements, and it became common for a simple page to contain hundreds or thousands of lines of spaghetti soup (unintelligible code). Listing 2-1 shows the same code example as in Chapter 1: a typical page's HTML code in practice, including lots of visual rendering instructions.

Listing 2-1. Typical HTML Code Before CSS and Modern Web Standards Were Widely Adopted

```
<FONT FACE=TIMES COLOR=#FF0000 SIZE=3>
 <H2><I>WELCOME TO MY WEBSITE</I></H2>
  <CENTER>
    <TABLE WIDTH=720 HEIGHT=480 BORDER=2 BGCOLOR=BLACK>
      <TR>
        <TD BACKGROUND=texture.gif>
          <TABLE WIDTH=360 HEIGHT=480 BORDER=0>
            <TR>
              <TD>
                <IMG SRC=spacer.gif WIDTH=360 HEIGHT=10><BR>
                  <H1>ABOUT MY SITE</H1>
                  <P>...</P>
              </TD>
            </TR>
          </TABLE>
        </TD>
        <TD BACKGROUND=texture2.gif>
          <TABLE WIDTH=360 HEIGHT=480 BORDER=0>
            <TR>
              <TD>
                <IMG SRC=spacer.gif WIDTH=360 HEIGHT=10><BR>
                  <H1>ABOUT ME</H1>
                  <P>...</P>
```

```
          </TD>
        </TR>
      </TABLE>
    </TD>
  </TR>
</TABLE>
</CENTER>
</FONT>
```

The issues raised by this approach to coding and maintaining web sites are obvious to everybody working with HTML. The Web needed a way to separate content from style, so the W3C took up the mantle, developing the CSS Level 1 specification.

Chapter 1 talked about the different visual characteristics CSS was designed to address. Recall that CSS Level 1 wasn't intended to act as a solution for layout. Instead, the idea was to replace all the basic visual characteristics that had been specified using HTML tags and attributes. As mentioned in Chapter 1, the result was a very limited set of properties covering the following:

- Width and height of block-level elements

- Float, and clear of floating elements

- Margins and padding

- Background colors and images

- Borders

- Fonts and font styles

- List styles

- Some basic alignment

CSS1 allowed designers to take the basic styling of individual elements outside the HTML code. For the first time, the way a web site looked could be controlled from a single, external file. This had massive benefits for the maintenance and consistency of page designs, because a single line of CSS code could now affect an entire web site. Previously, a simple heading color change meant editing every page of a web site individually.

It took web browsers some time to adopt the new CSS specification, and it wasn't until the late 1990s that designers could rely on the commonly used browsers to understand and render their CSS code with anything close to accuracy. For the history buffs, this was also the time when Microsoft and Netscape were battling for supremacy, with Internet Explorer the eventual victor.

It's worth noting that although you may be familiar with the idea of using floating elements as a system for creating layout, the `float` and `clear` properties introduced with CSS1 were never intended for this purpose. They were introduced to provide a CSS facsimile of the ALIGN=LEFT and ALIGN=RIGHT properties that were previously part of HTML, and were intended to be used on images, allowing text to flow around elements automatically.

Layout in CSS2 and CSS2.1

CSS2.1 introduced and defined four different layout modes for rendering web pages. These are systems the browser uses when parsing CSS rules to determine the size and position of elements based on their siblings, flow in the document, and parent elements. These four modes are as follows:

- *Block layout*: For laying out or organizing elements within a document

- *Inline layout*: For laying out text

- *Table layout*: For presenting and laying out tabular data in a two-dimensional grid

- *Positioned layout*: For explicitly positioning elements on the page, removing them from the document flow

Block Layout

The W3C's CSS2.1 specification offers this explanation of block layout:

> *In a block formatting context, boxes are laid out one after the other, vertically, beginning at the top of a containing block. The vertical distance between two sibling boxes is determined by the 'margin' properties. Vertical margins between adjacent block-level boxes in a block formatting context collapse.*

Block layout creates rectangular boxes around elements, which describe the amount of space occupied by that element. Many HTML elements automatically assume a block layout, including the likes of the `<p>`, `<h1>`, `<div>`, and `<ul>` elements. Block-level boxes stack vertically, with each occupying the vertical space immediately after the previous. Block-level boxes do not stack horizontally. Each new block appears in a new vertical position.

There are some special rules associated with the layout of block-level boxes, and rules that are applied to determine how much space each occupies. Briefly, these rules are as follows:

- The background of a block-level element extends fully to the outer edge of the border. This means the background fills both the content area and the combination of padding and border areas. If the border uses any transparency (for example, if it uses a dashed line), the background is visible in the space between the dashes.

- The width of a block-level element is set to auto by default (filling the available horizontal space). The only other attributes that can be set to auto are the margin and height properties.

- Negative values can be applied to the margin properties, but no other attributes can have a negative value.

- The width and height properties define the content area only. padding, border, and margin all add to the width of the box for the purposes of layout.

This is best illustrated with a diagram, as shown in Figure 2-2. margin, padding, and border all add to the displacement size of the block-level element. On a historical note, Internet Explorer's original implementation of the box model included the padding within the defined width (and height) of an element, leading to years of workarounds and browser-specific stylesheet hacks. Fortunately, those days are all but gone!

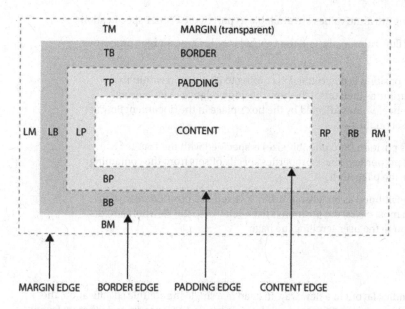

Figure 2-2. *The block-level box model. The* width *property affects only the content area, with padding, border, and* margin *adding to the overall displacement width and height*

Inline Layout

Inline-level elements are those elements of the source document that do not form new blocks of content; the content is distributed in lines (for example, emphasized pieces of text within a paragraph, inline images, and so on). Inline-level elements generate inline-level boxes, which are boxes that participate in an inline formatting context. This means they displace adjacent content in the same reading flow, but they don't interfere with block-level rendering.

An inline box is inline level, and its contents participate in its containing inline formatting context. A non-replaced element with a `display` value of `inline` generates an inline box. Common examples of elements that assume an inline behavior by default include `<span>` and `<em>`.

Table Layout

Accessed using the `display` attribute, table layout allows elements to act as if they form part of a table—assuming the role of a table cell, and occupying rows and/or columns within a tabular layout. This layout schema is incredibly powerful for all the same reasons that tables themselves were hijacked by early web designers, but poor browser support historically meant it never took off as a reliable layout solution.

Modern browser support is very good. As a result, table layout is a viable and valid layout approach to use.

Positioned Layout

Positioned layout lets you place individual elements precisely using coordinates, relative to the page or another containing element that has a defined position. This allows you to place an element in the top-right corner of the browser window or have individual elements overlapping each other in arbitrary positions within the viewport, as well as assuming a place in the document flow as is the default behavior.

Several different positioning attribute values are available as part of the CSS2.1 specification:

- *Static*: The normal flow rules apply, and the top, bottom, left, and right properties have no effect.

- *Relative*: The box's position is determined according to its position within the document flow. Attributes then offset the box's position relative to its "normal" position. Subsequent elements affected by the box's place in the document flow act as if there is no offset on the box.

- *Absolute*: The box's position (and possibly size) is specified with the top, left, bottom, and right properties. These properties specify offsets from the containing box (which may be the page itself).

- *Fixed*: The box is positioned as per absolute, but it's fixed in a position relative to some reference. In most cases, the position is fixed relative to the viewport and does not move in relation to the user scrolling the page.

Layout in CSS3

As already discussed, CSS3 handles layout in a new way. Instead of a single monolithic specification, the individual components are broken out into separate modules. As a result, CSS3 has several different layout modules, each of which is developed and maintained separately.

Several modules are already well supported in browsers; others are still being developed and defined. This book examines all the major layout modules and points out which ones you can use straight away and which are upcoming or ones to watch for the future. Chapter 1 briefly talked about each of these modules, so rather than cover each in detail again, here's a reminder of the modules this book looks at:

- CSS Multi-columns Layout

- CSS Flexible Box Layout (Flexbox)

- CSS Grid Layout

- CSS Regions Layout

This list isn't the limit of layout in CSS3, however. As you see toward the end of this book, some exciting ideas are being discussed and proposed that may change the way you lay out pages by default!

It's important to understand that CSS3 doesn't in any way replace CSS2.1 or CSS1. The new modules covered in the coming chapters build on top of the existing specification. As a result, you'll continue to use the four types of layout CSS2.1 introduced—block, inline, table, and absolute—as the most common, default layout solution. You can use these original layout paradigms in combination with, and to complement, the new modules.

The Importance of Going Modular

You may wonder why it's important that CSS3 is constructed in a modular fashion and how this is different than the way the existing CSS specification works. The quick answer is that by adopting a modular approach, each individual module that makes up CSS3 can be tested, evaluated, and adopted by browser vendors without the need to adopt the entire specification. It also means the CCSWG can focus on different areas of the specification in different stages in their lifecycle.

Why is this useful? Well, new layout modules that remain in development (for example, CSS Regions Layout and CSS Flexbox), can coexist alongside completed modules. Functionality can be released on an ongoing basis without the requirement that every module be completed, thereby increasing the speed of implementation and adoption. This is good for everyone!

I mentioned that different parts of the CSS3 specification are covered by different modules, and each of these is at a different stage in the development lifecycle. It sounds like the ideal solution, but it doesn't mean all the frustrating bits of developing a new specification are automatically removed. There's still an inherently slow development cycle, which can be frustrating to web designers and developers keen to move the Web forward.

What you can take away from this, however, is that different elements of the overall specification are available to use today. In contrast, it took CSS2.1 over a decade to become fully supported—and that was after all the development work had been completed within the CSS team at the W3C!

An additional benefit is that because each module is separate from the others, as one reaches maturity, the browser vendors (such as Microsoft, Apple, Google, and Opera) are able to integrate support it in their browsers. This provides early support for new modules and properties but does tend to come at a cost; because each new module is incomplete when the engineers are working to create support in the browser, new properties typically require a vendor-specific prefix before their declaration. This enables browsers to create early support without causing a problem with backward compatibility later: when the final specification is agreed on, the vendor prefix is removed, leaving only the completed specification property name and behavior.

To summarize, CSS3 is still in a state of flux (I'll remind you of this throughout this book!). Whereas with CSS2.1, the entire specification was contained in a single module, with CSS3, the individual components have been modularized. This means the CSSWG can iterate individual modules more quickly and efficiently, and browser vendors can implement standards without having to wait for every individual module to reach recommendation status.

Limitations of CSS Layout

As you've seen, CSS2.1 provides quite a few very useful layout options, and CSS3 brings a raft of new options to the toolbox. This is great news for web designers, and you're at the beginning of an exciting journey of discovery as new techniques are developed that take full advantage of the opportunities the new modules provide.

It's not all a bed of roses, though! There are still plenty of things that can't be done easily in CSS alone. For the majority of these tasks, scripted workarounds provide a solution; but complete layout nirvana is still a way off. The final chapters of this book take a whistle-stop tour of some upcoming proposals.

As you've seen, CSS is primarily concerned with the aesthetic presentation of a page, whether that's through the visual representation of content on screen, the way a page prints on the office laser printer, or how a screen reader accentuates the content. For this task, CSS is the best solution available to web designers and will be for the foreseeable future. If all you ever wanted to do was to create static web pages and render them beautifully, CSS would be exactly the right tool for the job.

As you may have guessed, there's a "but" coming! It's rare in today's web sites to find a page that doesn't require some kind of Document Object Model (DOM) manipulation (where elements in the tree are moved, added, or deleted) or procedurally generated markup. Sometimes you create pages that are rendered entirely through a server-side scripting language such as ASP.NET or PHP, using processing logic to generate a page that is rendered and styled on demand.

CSS can handle this scenario admirably, offering the flexibility to work with different quantities or arrangement of markup easily. What it's not designed for, however, is the case where designers attempt to reduce or remove the need to post back to the server to conduct data processing.

Let's take the example of a page with a search form that returns results as the user starts to type. Instead of relying on all content being rendered at the point where the page loads for the first time, you must now consider the idea that content may change at any time in response to new content being loaded dynamically.

■ **Note**   Before going any further, I should point out that these kind of interactive data-reactive user interface solutions post back to the server just as frequently as (and often more so) than the traditional page load/page render model. It's the method for generating and rendering content that has changed.

Content is normally loaded this way using either JSON or XML, courtesy of JavaScript. The script calls a server method that either generates additional markup for the page being read or outputs data in a format that can be interpreted by the script and used to manipulate the contents of the page.

Whichever way content is loaded, the amount and type of data shown on a page changes in response to an event. Of course, you can take every possible scenario into consideration when creating your stylesheet, but some nuances of presentation and demonstrating to the user that new content has been loaded into the page can't be achieved with CSS alone.

For these cases, JavaScript is the best way to manipulate the appearance of a page. Typically, JavaScript is used to update the CSS being applied to a specific element, but it's the ability to procedurally generate values and properties that differentiates a scripted solution from a native CSS-only approach.

In the cases where a particular layout can't be achieved with CSS alone, it's now perfectly acceptable to use JavaScript to provide a *polyfill* for the missing behavior. I cover these scenarios toward the end of each module's chapter.

■ **Note**   Just a reminder: some of the modules this book looks at are in a state of flux. Always check the W3C web site for the latest specification to ensure that you're working with the latest syntax.

Summary: Get Ready for the Future!

This chapter examined the layout options offered by the various levels of CSS. CSS1 brought primarily styling options for content, ignoring the need to control the position of those elements. Level 2 brought four distinct layout approaches for positioning elements relative to the page and each other. CSS3 goes far, far beyond these four tools.

Now, let's get on with learning about the new modules and how they can be used to create new layouts that weren't possible previously with CSS alone. The next chapter shows you a high-level overview of the pre-CSS3 layout modules in action, and after that it's CSS3 all the way. Let's get cracking!

CHAPTER 3

■ ■ ■

Where We've Been: Position, Float, and Display

This chapter introduces the CSS2.1 and CSS1 layout modules. It is intended as both a recap of the existing layout options and a best-practice tutorial/reference guide for the "old-fashioned" approach to CSS-based layout. Experienced web designers may choose to skip this chapter, but you'll potentially miss out on a few useful techniques and approaches that even the most hardened web designer may not be aware of. The chapter covers the following:

- Introduction to CSS layouts

- The CSS2.1 layout modules

- How to use them

- Real-world examples

You take a quick tour of all the layout paradigms that CSS offers, starting with the original version of CSS: Level 1. Note that each of the layout solutions offered by CSS has been implemented as a module. Up until CSS3 the entire CSS specification for each level was contained in an all-encompassing module, whereas each is now split into its own separate module; for simplicity, I talk about each approach as if it were a separate module.

As mentioned in Chapter 1, pre-CSS, HTML didn't offer much in the way of layout control. Designers found an ingenious method to craft sophisticated layouts: hacking the HTML specification by using tables to position elements precisely on the page. Tables were a very useful layout tool, because they offered a controllable solution to the positioning of individual pieces of content. HTML tables, however, were never intended to be used for layout; so, semantically speaking, the hack was a disaster. As the entire approach was a workaround, there were also issues of maintainability and readability of content. It wasn't uncommon to find nested tables six or seven levels deep.

With the arrival of CSS1, the focus started to shift away from rendering everything using HTML. Instead, the idea of separating content from the aesthetic presentation was established.

■ **Note** If you're already an expert with CSS2 layout, this chapter won't offer you any new insights, so feel free to move straight to Chapter 4. If you're new to web design, read on for a whistle-stop tour of the layout options offered by CSS2 and CSS1.

© Sam Hampton-Smith 2016
S. Hampton-Smith, *Pro CSS3 Layout Techniques*, DOI 10.1007/978-1-4302-6503-0_3

Layout Before CSS3

As mentioned in Chapter 2, HTML wasn't designed for layout beyond the ability to mark up content according to semantic hierarchy. The first version of the Web was simply a collection of scientific documents that linked to each other for easy access and retrieval. The HTML language did develop to incorporate some limited layout options in the form of alignment, but it was mainly through the misappropriation of the `<table>` tag that layout was achieved in the earliest days.

Picture the scene: you want to create a layout for the Web that features more than a single run of content like a Word document. Your design calls for two columns (a sidebar, in modern parlance). This wasn't practically possible using straight HTML, until somebody noticed that the `<table>` tag offered exactly this degree of layout control. Figure 3-1 shows a layout without any "layout," alongside a layout that uses tables to create a "layout." It's easy to see which is more visually attractive—it's little wonder designers pulled out every trick they could to beautify and push the boundaries of web design.

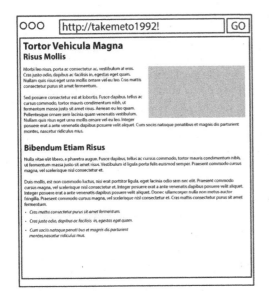
Without any "layout"

Layout produced with HTML `<table>`

Figure 3-1. *A linear layout versus a table-based layout, demonstrating the attraction of using tables when there were no other options available to designers*

By using tables to arrange different bits of content, designers were able to precisely control the position of elements on the page. This was despite the idea that tables were designed for presenting tabular data sets. This approach worked for a time, but as designers began to seek out more progressive designs, the `<table>` layout revolution turned sour. Incredibly intricate layouts are possible using tables, but the more intricate the design, the more likely it is to require tables within tables and cells that span multiple columns or rows; this leads to a terrible case of spaghetti code that is difficult to decipher and horrible to maintain.

The issue of unintelligible code wasn't unique to tables, however. As part of a wider strategy to separate style from content, the W3C worked to design CSS. It wasn't until CSS2 that any layout-specific features became available; this chapter introduces these features.

Chapter 2 listed the layout paradigms. This chapter talks about all the options from a practical use point of view, so let's add floated layout to that list. The available CSS layout options before the arrival of CSS3 were as follows:

- *Block layout*: For controlling boxes when laying out documents

- *Inline layout*: For laying out text

- *Table layout*: For presenting and laying out tabular data in a two-dimensional grid

- *Relative and positioned layout*: Allows elements to be explicitly positioned on the page, either reacting to the flow of the document and impacting subsequent elements, or removing them from the document flow and causing them to have no impact on surrounding elements on the page

- *Floated layout*: Allows elements to be removed from the document flow at the point they occur but still impact on relatively positioned elements on the page

If you're scratching your head at table layout, that's understandable. There was never an issue with the idea behind using tables for layout, but the HTML table implementation wasn't designed to accommodate layout. So the CSS 2.1 specification introduced table layout as a layout paradigm. Let's look at each of these options for achieving layout, including some basic examples to help you hit the ground running if you're new to layout on the Web.

Relative and Absolute Positioning

By default, HTML elements on a page adopt *relative positioning*. This means they push other elements out the way to make the space they need to occupy their position within the document. If you choose to assign absolute positioning to an element, you remove that element from the normal document flow, and it no longer jostles for position with the other elements on the page. Additionally, whereas relatively positioned elements are placed on the page as a result of the preceding elements on the page, absolutely positioned elements can be assigned coordinates to occupy. Have a look at the code in Listing 3-1 to see both options in action.

Listing 3-1. Difference between Relative and Absolute Positioning

```
<style>
.relative {
 position: relative;
 width: 100px;
 height: 100px;
 background: red;
 margin: 10px;
}
.absolute {
 position: absolute;
 top: 100px;
 left: 200px;
 width: 100px;
 height: 100px;
 background: yellow;
 margin: 10px;
}
```

```
</style>
<div class="relative">Element 1</div>
<div class="relative">Element 2</div>
<div class="relative">Element 3</div>
<div class="absolute">Element 4</div>
<div class="absolute">Element 5</div>
<div class="absolute">Element 6</div>
```

The result of Listing 3-1 is shown in Figure 3-2: the relatively positioned elements are neatly stacked one above the other, with a 10px gap introduced thanks to the `margin` property. The absolutely positioned elements, however, are all stacked on top of one another, so you can only see the most recently painted element (element 6). This is an example of *z-index*, a property you can set on elements to change the order in which they appear in the stack of elements on the page and, by extension, the order in which they're painted.

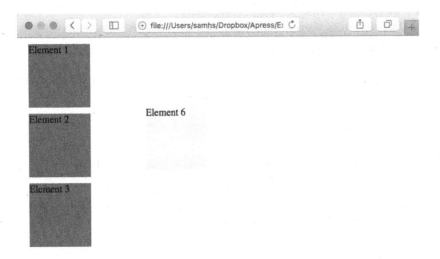

Figure 3-2. *The result of the code in Listing 3-1*

Absolutely positioned elements offer a great deal of fine control, but they're not always handy when you're dealing with different-sized screens and browser windows. Often you'll want the document flow to dictate where elements appear on the page. It's worth being aware, then, that absolute positioning uses coordinates relative to its parent element. This means if you place an absolutely positioned element inside a relatively positioned element, the absolutely positioned element moves to reflect the position of the parent. Handy!

Look at the example code shown in Listing 3-2 to see how this works in practice. The result is shown in Figure 3-3. Note that absolutely positioned elements can render outside the bounds of their relative parent. The parent simply provides the anchor point from which the positioning is calculated. It's also worth highlighting that the final absolutely positioned element in this example is sitting not within a relatively positioned `<div>`, but rather the relatively positioned `<body>`: it appears to render higher up the page because the positioning coordinates are calculated from the top left of the page overall, rather than an element sitting somewhere else on the page.

Listing 3-2. An elaboration on the previous example, showing the difference between relative and absolute positioning

```
<style>
.relative {
 position: relative;
 top: 100px;
 left: 100px;
 width: 100px;
 height: 100px;
 background: red;
 margin: 10px;
}
#absolute1 {
 position: absolute;
 top: 100px;
 left: 200px;
 width: 100px;
 height: 100px;
 background: yellow;
}
#absolute2 {
 position: absolute;
 top: 100px;
 left: 200px;
 width: 100px;
 height: 100px;
 background: purple;
}
#absolute3 {
 position: absolute;
 top: 100px;
 left: 200px;
 width: 100px;
 height: 100px;
 background: yellow;
}
</style>
<div class="relative">
 Element 1
 <div id="absolute1">Element 4</div>
</div>
<div class="relative">Element 2</div>
<div class="relative">
 Element 3
 <div id="absolute2">Element 5</div>
</div>
<div id="absolute3">Element 6</div>
```

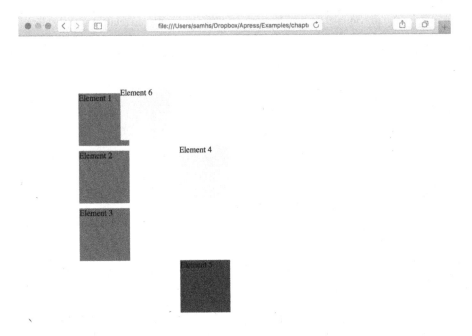

Figure 3-3. *The result of the code in Listing 3-2*

A combination of both relative and absolute positioning can offer a good solution to many different layout challenges on the Web, but by no means all of them. Take the earlier example where a designer wants to incorporate a sidebar into a page. An absolutely positioned element could give the impression of a sidebar, but because absolute positioning removes an element from the document flow, the sidebar wouldn't respect any other content on the page. It would obscure any content that wanted to render beneath it, and it wouldn't react to any other content areas around it. In these circumstances, designers turned to floating elements instead.

Floated Layout

Floated elements do exactly that: they float within their parent element, either to the left or to the right. No content within the parent element can infringe on the space occupied by the floating element. Instead, content flows around the floating element, allowing it to continue to impact surrounding elements. Note, however, that floating an element removes it from the sizing flow of the page.

As with positioning elements absolutely within a relative element, floats don't need to remain within the confines of the parent element (although they do remain as such on the horizontal axis). Why is this a problem? Because floating elements can leak out the bottom of a relatively positioned element, impacting the positioning of subsequent relatively positioned elements on the page.

Let's see an example of this effect in action. Listing 3-3 shows a basic floating element sitting in a relatively positioned parent. Listing 3-4 expands on the layout, adding additional floating elements such that they overflow the bottom of the parent element. Figure 3-4 shows the result of Listing 3-3, and Figure 3-5 shows the result of Listing 3-4.

Listing 3-3. Continuing to explore the differences between Relative and Absolute Positioning

```
<style>
.relative {
 position: relative;
 width: 300px;
 background: grey;
 margin: 10px;
 padding: 10px;
}
#floater {
 float: right;
 width: 160px;
 height: 160px;
 padding: 10px;
 margin: 10px;
 background: green;
}
</style>
<div class="relative">
  <div id="floater">Floating element</div>
  <p>Cras justo odio, dapibus ac facilisis in, egestas eget quam. Etiam porta sem malesuada
  magna mollis euismod. Vestibulum id ligula porta felis euismod semper. Fusce dapibus,
  tellus ac cursus commodo, tortor mauris condimentum nibh, ut fermentum massa justo sit
  amet risus.</p>
</div>
```

Listing 3-4. Floating Element within a Relative Parent: Content within the Relative Element Flows around the Floating Element

```
<style>
.relative {
 position: relative;
 width: 300px;
 background: grey;
 margin: 10px;
 padding: 10px;
}
.floater {
 float: right;
 width: 160px;
 height: 160px;
 padding: 10px;
 margin: 10px;
 background: green;
}
```

```
</style>
<div class="relative">
  <div class="floater">Floating element 1</div>
  <div class="floater">Floating element 2</div>
  <div class="floater">Floating element 3</div>
  <div class="floater">Floating element 4</div>
  <p>Cras justo odio, dapibus ac facilisis in, egestas eget quam. Etiam porta sem malesuada
magna mollis euismod. Vestibulum id ligula porta felis euismod semper. Fusce dapibus, tellus ac
cursus commodo, tortor mauris condimentum nibh, ut fermentum massa justo sit amet risus.</p>
</div>
```

Figure 3-4. *The result of Listing 3-3*

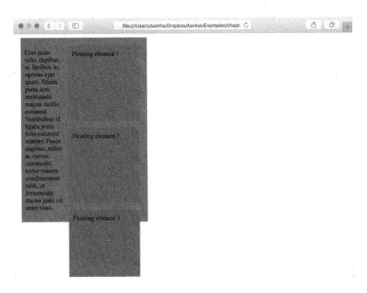

Figure 3-5. *The result of Listing 3-4. Note how floating elements do not contribute to the height of the relatively positioned parent element*

Floated elements were commonly used to create horizontal navigation bars in the days prior to CSS3. But as you'll see, there are new and exciting (and much more reliable) options coming up in CSS3.

The biggest issue with floats is that they're unpredictable. There are workarounds, as shown in Listing 3-5, which uses the clear property to instruct an element to appear only after all floated elements have finished rendering. But these workarounds tend to lead to superfluous code or redundant elements on the page, such as a <br> tag being used solely for the purpose of expanding a relatively positioned element to fully enclose a floated child. It's also worth saying again that floated elements don't impact on structural layout, so a sidebar created using a floated element can't be matched for height with its parent element without resorting to hacks or scripts.

Listing 3-5. Using the clear Property to Ensure that the Second Floating Element Doesn't Stack Next to the First

```
<style>
.relative {
 position: relative;
 width: 300px;
 background: grey;
 margin: 10px;
 padding: 10px;
}
.floater {
 float: right;
 width: 60px;
 height: 60px;
 padding: 10px;
 margin: 10px;
 background: green;
}
.clearfloat {
 clear: right;
}
</style>
<div class="relative">
  <div class="floater">Floating element 1</div>
  <div class="floater clearfloat">Floating element 2</div>
  <div class="floater">Floating element 3</div>
  <div class="floater ">Floating element 4</div>
  <p>Cras justo odio, dapibus ac facilisis in, egestas eget quam. Etiam porta sem malesuada
  magna mollis euismod. Vestibulum id ligula porta felis euismod semper. Fusce dapibus,
  tellus ac cursus commodo, tortor mauris condimentum nibh, ut fermentum massa justo sit
  amet risus.</p>
  <br class="clearfloat" /> <!-- this isn't necessary on this page, but is commonly used to
  ensure the <div> with a class of relative expands to encapsulate the floating elements -->
</div>
```

Figure 3-6 shows the result of Listing 3-5. The clear property forces the surrounding elements to take floats into account; but as you can see in the last line of code, this can lead to additional elements being introduced into the markup solely for the purpose of working around the limitations of floats. This isn't a good thing! CSS is, after all, designed to promote the separation of style and content.

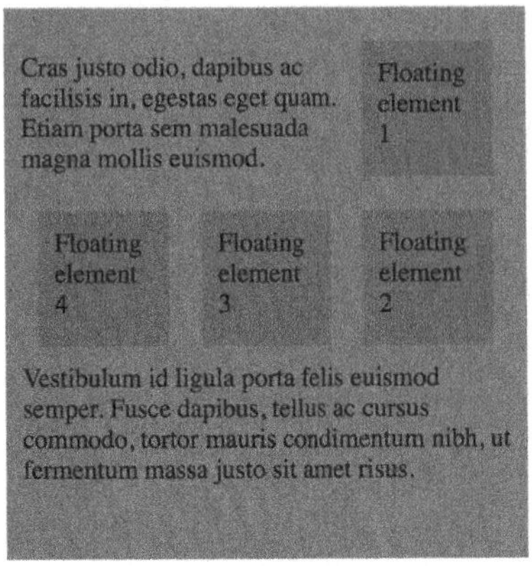

Figure 3-6. *The output of Listing 3-5*

Caveats aside, floated elements definitely have their uses. Images that appear within blocks of text, pull quotes, in-section navigation, and asides are all valid uses for the float property, so don't discount it as a tool in your layout arsenal.

Everything this chapter has talked about until this point relies on the element in question having some size and position on the page. This is known as *block display*, and that's what the next section talks about.

Block and Inline Display

There are two different types of display for elements on a page, and the default display style for any particular element depends on its semantic function. Let's look at what each term means:

- *Block display* means the element occupies horizontal and vertical space, with an invisible bounding box enclosing it. Block elements displace other elements on the page, causing them to shift position to accommodate the space of their bounding box. Block-level elements always start in a new vertical space and occupy the full width available, stretching as far as they can.

- *Inline display* means the element sits within the flow of content, occupying horizontal space but not impacting vertical layout except any displacement caused by the element's proportions.

The diagram in Figure 3-7 shows the differences between the two types of display.

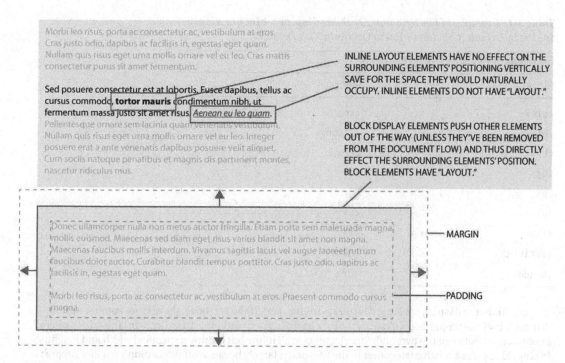

Figure 3-7. *Differences between block and inline display, and how each impacts layout*

■ **Note**   Keep in mind that when I say *vertical* and *horizontal*, I'm assuming you're working in a Latin left-to-right, top-to-bottom language. CSS now supports other reading directions, too, but to avoid confusion I'm using the terms as synonyms for the reading direction in use on the page.

There's another type of display you haven't seen: *none*. If you set the display property to none, the element remains on the page but ceases to be painted by the rendering engine or cause any displacement to surrounding elements. You may wonder when you would want to use display: none, because surely it would make more sense to exclude the HTML code rather than use CSS to hide the element. Think in terms of pop-up modal dialogs, "read more" sections of pages, and drop-down menu systems. Setting the display property to a value of none is an incredibly useful power to be able to wield, and much of the interaction you encounter on the Web wouldn't be possible without it! (If you really need to hide an element but still have it occupy the space it would on the page, use visibility: hidden instead of display: none. When you're ready to show it again, use visibility: visible. This continues to render the object but prevents it from being painted on screen, allowing it to continue to take up space in the layout.)

Let's look at some examples of block and inline elements. Table 3-1 shows some common examples of each.

Table 3-1. *Examples of Elements that Are Either* display: block *or* display: inline *by Default (CSS Allows You to Overwrite This Default)*

Examples of Block and Inline Elements

Block	Inline
<div>	<span>
<h1>	<strong>
<h2>	<em>
<h3>	<i>
<p>	
<ul>	<u>
<li>	<a>
<article>	<abbr>
<header>	

In addition to display: block, display: inline, and display: none, there is yet another option that combines the properties of display: block and display: inline. Display: inline-block offers a compromise between the two, allowing elements to sit inline but occupy a specified width and height. Inline-block was a relative latecomer to the CSS party, largely because browsers didn't reliably support it in the early days of CSS2.1. As a result, it's not as common in page designs; but it's another valuable tool and an option to help solve layout challenges. Listing 3-6 shows a simple example of display: inline-block in action. The result is shown in Figure 3-8.

Listing 3-6. Using inline-block to Give Inline Elements Structure in the Form of Width and Height

```
<style>
.relative {
 position: relative;
 padding: 10px;
 width: 500px;
 background: red;
 margin: 10px;
}
.navitem {
  display: inline-block;
  width: 70px;
  height: 40px;
  line-height: 40px;
  text-align: center;
  background: grey
}
</style>
```

```
<div class="relative">
  <h1>Example of inline-block</h1>
  <p>Here is some content <span>that includes an inline &lt;span&gt; element</span>.</p>
  <p>Here's some more content, and this time the &lt;span&gt; elements have the class
  navitem applied to them: <span class="navitem">Item 1</span> <span class="navitem">
  Item 2</span> <span class="navitem">Item 3</span></p>
  <p>Note that inline-block elements contribute to the layout.</p>
</div>
```

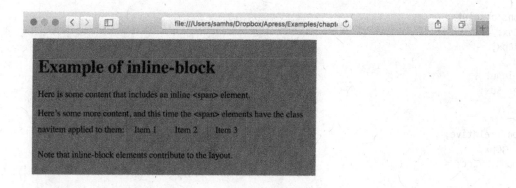

Figure 3-8. *The output of Listing 3-6, where elements have been given structure thanks to* `display: inline-block`

How Does the Display Property Impact Layout?

As you've seen, you have a lot of control over the way elements are drawn on the page. The `display` property directly affects layout. By default, some elements' `width` and `height` can't be explicitly set, and thus cannot they can't impact surrounding elements or their position on the page. Others have an impact by default. Naturally, you can override the default property for any element using the `display` property in CSS.

Let's have a quick look at this in action. Listing 3-7 combines relative and absolute positioning; floating elements; and inline, block, and inline-block elements into a single page. This isn't uncommon; you'll typically find examples of every kind of layout in most complicated layouts. The result of Listing 3-7 is shown in Figure 3-9.

Listing 3-7. Combining relative, absolute, `float`, `inline`, `block`, and `inline-block` Elements into One Example Layout

```
<style>
.relative {
  padding: 10px;
  position: relative;
  width: 920px;
  background: #efefef;
  border: 1px solid #ccc;
  margin: 10px auto;
}
```

```css
#header {
 position: relative;
 padding: 10px;
 height: 80px;
 line-height: 80px;
 background: #999;
 color: #fff
}
#header h1 { font-weight: normal;margin:0;padding:0;}
#search {
 position: absolute;
 top: 10px;
 right:10px;
}
#search input {
 padding: 5px;
}
#nav {
 position: relative;
 height: 30px;
 background: #ccc;
}
#nav ul {
 margin: 0;
 padding: 0;
}
#nav ul li {
 float: left;
 list-style:none;
 padding: 0;
 margin: 0 3px;
 width: 70px;
 height: 30px;
 line-height: 30px;
 text-align: center;
 background: #ddd;
}
.sidebar {
 float: right;
 width: 200px;
 background: #ebebeb;
 padding: 10px;
}
.ib {
 display: inline-block;
 width: 70px;
 line-height: 30px;
 text-align: center;
 background: #ddd;
 border: #ccc;
 margin: 5px;
```

```
}
.clearfloat {
  clear: both;
}
</style>

<div class="relative">
 <div id="header">
  <h1>Site Name</h1>
  <form id="search"><input type="text" value="search site" /></form>
 </div>
 <div id="nav">
  <ul>
   <li><a href="#">Home</a></li>
   <li><a href="#">About</a></li>
   <li><a href="#">Contact</a></li>
  </ul>
 </div>
 <div class="sidebar">
  <h3>Popular CSS modules</h3>
  <p><span class="ib">CSS Flexbox</span><span class="ib">CSS Multi-Column</span><span
  class="ib">CSS Regions</span><span class="ib">CSS Grid Layout</span><span class="ib">CSS
  Shapes</span></p>
 </div>
 <div id="content">
  <h2>Welcome to our website</h2>
  <p>Praesent commodo cursus magna, vel scelerisque nisl consectetur et. Curabitur blandit
  tempus porttitor. Maecenas faucibus mollis interdum. Aenean eu leo quam. Pellentesque
  ornare sem lacinia quam venenatis vestibulum.</p>
  <p>Donec id elit non mi porta gravida at eget metus. Vivamus sagittis lacus vel augue
  laoreet rutrum faucibus dolor auctor. Curabitur blandit tempus porttitor. Donec sed odio
  dui. Maecenas sed diam eget risus varius blandit sit amet non magna.</p>
  <p>Praesent commodo cursus magna, vel scelerisque nisl consectetur et. Donec id elit
  non mi porta gravida at eget metus. Praesent commodo cursus magna, vel scelerisque nisl
  consectetur et. Nulla vitae elit libero, a pharetra augue.</p>
  <p>Sed posuere consectetur est at lobortis. Sed posuere consectetur est at lobortis.
  Maecenas sed diam eget risus varius blandit sit amet non magna. Nullam id dolor id nibh
  ultricies vehicula ut id elit.</p>
 </div>
 <br class="clearfloat" />
</div>
```

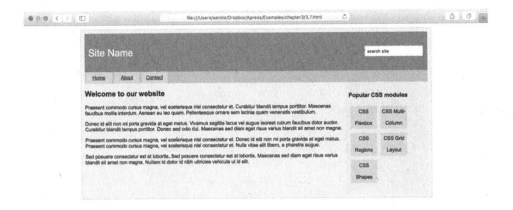

Figure 3-9. *The output of Listing 3-7. Note that different layout paradigms are suited to different solutions, so it's common to use a range of tools to achieve a specific part of the overall layout*

Table Layout

The last layout tool this chapter examines is table layout. As you saw in Chapters 1 and 2, tables have been used since the earliest days of the Web to achieve layout. Once CSS became available and reliable, there was a strong anti-table-layout movement on the Web, and as a result table layout has almost become taboo. This is an opinion formed on the basis of tables in HTML being solely for the use of tabular data, rather than layout and display of a page.

It's important, then, to draw a distinction between HTML tables and CSS tables. The table layout discussed here is achieved by assigning `display: table` to a container element. The difference between applying `display: table` to an existing page element and using an HTML `<table>` element is that by definition, a `<table>` element is and always will be a table. A `<div>` with `display: table` set as a property can be changed to use a different layout paradigm simply by editing the CSS code or using an `@media` query. CSS tables are good for layout!

CSS table layout offers a style-based solution to rendering content in a manner that's manner to HTML tables but not identical. The corresponding property values for each different table element are as follows:

- `table`   `{ display: table }`
- `tr`   `{ display: table-row }`
- `thead`   `{ display: table-header-group }`
- `tbody`   `{ display: table-row-group }`
- `tfoot`   `{ display: table-footer-group }`
- `col`   `{ display: table-column }`
- `colgroup` `{ display: table-column-group }`
- `td, th`   `{ display: table-cell }`
- `caption` `{ display: table-caption }`

Listing 3-8 shows how each of these can be used to achieve a table-based layout, with all the benefits that approach provides. The result is shown in Figure 3-10.

Listing 3-8. Creating a Layout Using display: table Properties to Achieve Something that's Very Difficult Using Alternative CSS2.1 Layout Options

```
<style>
.table {
  display: table;
  border: 1px solid red;
  background: #eee;
  margin: 2px;
  padding: 2px;
}
.tr {
  display: table-row;
  border: 1px solid red;
  background: #ddd;
  margin: 2px;
  padding: 2px;
}
.td {
  display: table-cell;
  border: 1px solid #red;
  width: 200px;
  background: #ccc;
  margin: 2px;
  padding: 2px;
}
</style>
<div class="table">
 <div class="tr">
  <div class="td"><p>This is a normal div, but displays like a cell in a table!</p></div>
  <div class="td"><p>This is another table cell</p></div>
 </div>
 <div class="tr">
  <div class="td"><p>Here is a third cell, in a second row</p></div>
  <div class="td"><p>And a final cell.</p></div>
 </div>
</div>
```

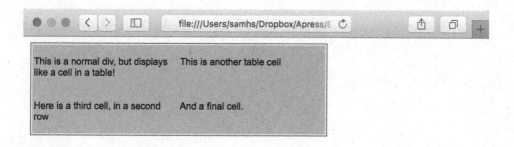

Figure 3-10. A page layout achieved using display: table. This is practically impossible to achieve without table layout, unless you use scripts or CSS3! Note that some properties have been ignored and aren't rendered in the final page. display: table works just like an HTML table!

CSS table layout is a very useful layout tool that is the best option in myriad scenarios. Before the arrival of CSS3, it was a good option to achieve a three-column layout where the individual columns matched the height of the longest column without the need for scripts or hacks. It's also a useful way to vertically align content without having to resort to negative margins and other such workarounds. But this book is about CSS3—let's not spend too much more time worrying about `display: table`. You may encounter it, and it's certainly not to be ignored as a potential layout tool, but you're not reading this book to find out about table-based layout!

This chapter's takeaway is that CSS layout modules don't exist in isolation. You're extremely unlikely to encounter a design that doesn't incorporate styling born out of the gamut of CSS layout options. Successful designers use the best tool for the job, so don't be afraid to call on CSS2.1 layout modules when designing a page. Find the layout module that works best for your specific requirements in a design element, and use that.

Summary

In this chapter, you've seen a high-level overview of the layout options available prior to CSS3. Some basic examples helped to explain the options, and the chapter also talked about some layout limitations using these modules. You will use all of these layout modules on a daily basis when designing web sites; so if your appetite is whetted and you want further reading, check out the Apress store for books that cover CSS2.1.

Now you're equipped to create layouts using CSS2.1. Let's get to the point and begin learning about the new stuff: it's time to explore CSS3 Layout!

CHAPTER 4

■ ■ ■

CSS Multi-column Layout

The CSS Multi-column Layout module provides a solution to one of the fundamental layout issues that has faced web designers since the very earliest days of the Web: how to arrange content so that it occupies multiple vertical containers, like a newspaper or magazine. Over the years, ingenious web designers have developed a variety of workarounds to create multi-column layouts. Initially this involved using tables to align columns of content as if each element was a value in a cell. More recently, clever combinations of floating elements, clearing elements, and occasional JavaScript have provided a more semantic solution, but none of these approaches is particularly well suited to creating multi-column layouts. The new CSS3 module overcomes many of the problems associated with generating such layouts, automatically handling the flow and distribution of content; and browser support is already quite good, so it's relatively safe to start using this module today!

■ **Note**   Although browser support is already good, this module is still being implemented by browser vendors. All the usual caveats apply!

What Is the CSS Multi-column Layout Module?

CSS Multi-column Layout provides a solution for dividing a content area into columns, across which content is automatically paginated. Unlike some of the other all-new layout modules covered in this book, the Multi-column Layout module extends the existing CSS box model. Because the new module builds on top of an existing layout paradigm, fallback is handled automatically. Browsers that don't understand multi-column layout properties ignore them, rendering the content area in a single column instead of as multiple columns; see Figure 4-1.

© Sam Hampton-Smith 2016
S. Hampton-Smith, *Pro CSS3 Layout Techniques*, DOI 10.1007/978-1-4302-6503-0_4

Figure 4-1. *CSS Multi-column Layout in action versus a fallback non-columnar layout in the same container*

Syntax and Structure

The CSS Multi-column Layout module extends the existing CSS box model with a total of ten additional properties. Each of these provides control over one aspect of the way content is rendered into columns within the container.

Because all the properties affect a single container, the module is both very easy to understand and, importantly, straightforward to implement from a browser point of view. As a result, "in the wild" support for this module is excellent! If your users are up to date with the latest build of their particular choice of browser, your content will render in columns—every commonly used browser supports this module.

■ **Note**   As with any of the new CSS3 layout modules, it's always worth thoroughly testing across all browser and operating system combinations. You can view the latest browser support table for CSS Multi-column at `http://caniuse.com/`.

Basic Concepts

The CSS3 Multi-column Layout module introduces ten new properties that can be applied to block-level elements. In addition to the new properties that control the number of columns, distribution, width, and divisions, some new keywords are available to help control how content breaks across columns.

Creating a multi-column layout is very simple with the Multi-column Layout module. There are no unnecessarily complicated properties to learn; and because everything happens in a single element, there's no need to worry about how content will wrap outside its container, beyond the rules you're familiar with from CSS2.1.

With just the ten properties, you can do the following:

- Convert an existing single-column element into a multi-column element

- Wrap content automatically across columns

- Control how columns fill the available space, either by expanding to fill the container or by always adhering to a preset size (which is handy for creating responsive layouts)

- Define the borders that appear between columns, and the gutter width

- Render content so that it spans multiple columns to break out of the columnar layout when desired

There are some special rules about how overflowing content is rendered and the way in which content breaks across columns. You learn about these in detail later in this chapter.

It's worth highlighting the third item in the list of things CSS Multi-column Layout lets you do. Right out of the box, CSS columns can be responsive. This means it's an ideal layout module to use if you want to target and paginate content for multiple different device configurations. There are ways you can break this in-built responsiveness, but the coming pages highlight what to watch out for.

The responsive nature of CSS columns isn't limited to text. Images also adhere to the column layout, so by using typical responsive image techniques, you can also make pictures scale to suit the screen being used to view a page. This is a great time-saver and another good reason it's worth your time to familiarize yourself with the module.

I hope you're convinced that CSS Multi-column Layout is a useful tool in your layout arsenal. Let's get into the code to see how it works.

Understanding the Terminology

Unlike some of the other layout modules covered in this book, the CSS Multi-column Layout module uses an existing layout paradigm that we're all familiar with. This makes it very easy to understand and to get started using the module in your layouts. With that said (and just in case you're not comfortable with the concept of what a column is), let's quickly cover what the word *column* means in the context of CSS.

A *column* is a vertical division in which content is rendered, inside an overall container. One container can contain one or more columns, with content flowing from one to the next according to the rules of the language being used. If you're authoring in English, columns render from left to right. As content overflows the first column, it starts being rendered at the top of the next column. When all the columns have been used, the content overflows according to the normal HTML/CSS rules, although this may result in additional columns—you look at this later.

One of the benefits of the CSS Multi-column module is that the height of the container is automatically calculated to accommodate all the content by default. This is useful and one of the major benefits of using the module over some of the older workaround solutions. Out of the box, content is also automatically balanced across all columns, resulting in a pleasing block of content delineated into neat columns to match your specification.

Figure 4-2 demonstrates the different properties used in the discussion of CSS Multi-column Layout. You'll probably pick this up quickly, because it's intuitive; but if you're ever unsure about the difference between `column-fill` and `column-span`, this figure will be worth referring back to.

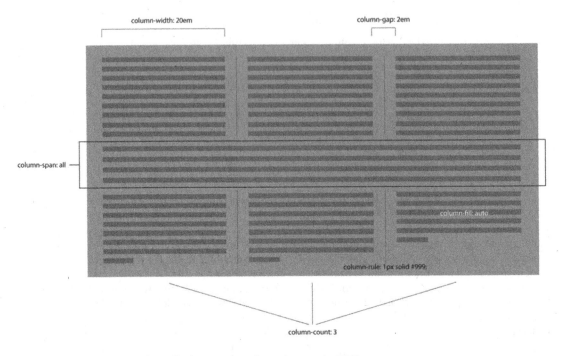

Figure 4-2. *The terms used to talk about multi-column layouts in CSS3*

Before getting engrossed in theory and property names/values, let's look at an example. The code for a basic multi-column layout is shown Listing 4-1, and you can see an example of the output in Figure 4-3. I'll explain what's going on in this example over the coming pages. Note that, as with all emerging modules that are implemented with vendor-prefixed properties, you may need to add -webkit- or -moz- prefixes to get this to display in your browser.

Listing 4-1. HTML Markup Being Styled with CSS Multi-column Layout Properties

```
<style>
.multicol {
  position:    relative;
  margin:      auto;
  max-width:   960px;
  columns:     4 12em;
  column-gap:  2em;
  column-rule: 1px solid red;
}
.multicol p {
  padding:     0.25em;
}
.multicol figure {
  margin:      0;
  padding:     0;
  width:       100%;
}
```

```
.multicol figcaption {
  color:      #999;
  font-size:      0.7em;
}
.multicol img {
  width:      100%;
}
.multicol h1 {
  column-span:      all;
  margin:      0.25em 0;
  padding:      0;
}
.multicol h2 {
  margin:      0.25em 0;
  padding:      0;
}
</style>

<article class="multicol">
  <h1>Moby Dick; Or the Whale</h1>
  <h2>by Herman Melville</h2>
  <figure>
    <img src="images/mobydick.jpg" alt="Cover of Moby Dick" />
    <figcaption>Voyage of the Pequod, illustrated by Everett Henry</figcaption>
  </figure>
  <p>Call me Ishmael. Some years ago—never mind how long precisely—having little or no money
  in my purse, and nothing particular to interest me on shore, I thought I would sail about
  a little ... How then is this? Are the green fields gone? What do they here?</p>
</article>
```

MOBY DICK; OR THE WHALE

BY HERMAN MELVILLE

Voyage of the Pequod, illustrated by Everett Henry

Call me Ishmael. Some years ago—never mind how long precisely—having little or no money in my purse, and nothing particular to interest me on shore, I thought I would sail about a little and see the watery part of the world. It is a way I have of driving off the spleen and regulating the circulation. Whenever I find myself growing grim about the mouth;

whenever it is a damp, drizzly November in my soul; whenever I find myself involuntarily pausing before coffin warehouses, and bringing up the rear of every funeral I meet; and especially whenever my hypos get such an upper hand of me, that it requires a strong moral principle to prevent me from deliberately stepping into the street, and methodically knocking people's hats off—then, I account it high time to get to sea as soon as I can. This is my substitute for pistol and ball. With a philosophical flourish Cato throws himself upon his sword; I quietly take to the ship. There is nothing surprising in this. If they but knew it,

almost all men in their degree, some time or other, cherish very nearly the same feelings towards the ocean with me.

There now is your insular city of the Manhattoes, belted round by wharves as Indian isles by coral reefs—commerce surrounds it with her surf. Right and left, the streets take you waterward. Its extreme downtown is the battery, where that noble mole is washed by waves, and cooled by breezes, which a few hours previous were out of sight of land. Look at the crowds of water-gazers there.

Circumambulate the city of a dreamy Sabbath

afternoon. Go from Corlears Hook to Coenties Slip, and from thence, by Whitehall, northward. What do you see?—Posted like silent sentinels all around the town, stand thousands upon thousands of mortal men fixed in ocean reveries. Some leaning against the spiles; some seated upon the pier-heads; some looking over the bulwarks of ships from China; some high aloft in the rigging, as if striving to get a still better seaward peep. But these are all landsmen; of week days pent up in lath and plaster —tied to counters, nailed to benches, clinched to desks. How then is this? Are the green fields gone? What do they here?

Figure 4-3. *The resulting appearance from the combination of HTML and CSS code in Listing 4-1, shown at normal desktop resolution of greater than 960px width*

The really useful thing about this example is that it's immediately responsive, as you can see in Figures 4-4 and 4-5, where I've reduced my browser window's width to simulate smaller screens. Let's look at the different elements of this example.

Figure 4-4. *The same rendering shown with a reduced browser window width*

MOBY DICK; OR THE WHALE

BY HERMAN MELVILLE

Voyage of the Pequod, illustrated by Everest Henry

Call me Ishmael. Some years ago—never mind how long precisely—having little or no money in my purse, and nothing particular to interest me on shore, I thought I would sail about a little and see the watery part of the world. It is a way I have of driving off the spleen and regulating the circulation. Whenever I find myself growing grim about the mouth; whenever it is a damp, drizzly November in my soul; whenever I find myself involuntarily pausing before coffin warehouses, and bringing up the rear of every funeral I meet; and especially whenever my hypos get such an upper hand of me, that it requires a strong moral principle to prevent me from deliberately stepping into the street, and methodically knocking people's hats off—then, I account it high time to get to sea as soon as I can. This is

Figure 4-5. *The result of Listing 4-1 rendered at 320px wide—the most common smartphone resolution*

■ **Note** Some additional non-multi-column-layout code is required to define the color, border, and typographic styles shown in Figures 4-3, 4-4, and 4-5. I've also abridged the paragraph content in the markup shown in Listing 4-1 to save space.

The HTML Markup

I don't need to talk about the HTML, because you're using a standard semantic element as the container for the content. There are no special markup requirements to use CSS Multi-column Layout; any block-level element can have multiple columns applied to it using this module.

The Multi-column Model

There are a few things to notice about the example shown in Figure 4-3 and Listing 4-1, specifically with regard to how the content renders in the container. In the original CSS box model, the content of an element flows into the content box of that element. CSS Multi-column Layout introduces a new type of container that exists between the content box and the actual content. This is referred to by the W3C as the *column box* (*column* for short). Content flows automatically across columns within an element, in the inline (or reading) direction. This is left-to-right in Latin-based languages such as English.

Columns are arranged into rows. All columns have a common width and height within a row. Columns can have space between them, which is referred to as the *column gap* (or *gutter* in print-speak). In most onscreen cases, an element split into columns has only a single row. There are, however, special cases where an element may contain multiple rows of columns. Printed documents can also consist of multiple rows, where a content area occupies more than one printed page. You see an example of multiple onscreen rows in action later in this chapter.

I use the W3C's language when explaining CSS3 Multi-column Layout Layout. For that reason, I refer to the multicol element when talking about the container that has the multi-column properties applied to it. A multi-column (multicol) element is any container whose column-width or column-count is not set to auto. As you've seen, in this case I'm using an <article> element. To avoid confusion, I also use multicol as the name of the class belonging to this element.

All the individual properties covered in the next section are applied to the multicol element. In CSS3, it isn't possible to set properties and values on individual columns. To be clear, this means you can't assign background, padding, or margin for one column specifically.

■ **Note**   Padding and margin applied to a multicol element are applied to the container, not its columns

---

Although you can't control individual columns, it's important to understand that the browser renderer treats them as separate block-level boxes just like table cells. Each column box acts as the containing block for its content. This means, for example, margin and padding applied to a paragraph element rendered in a column are applied against the edge of that column's containing block.

The CSS Properties

Looking at the CSS code for the example shown in Listing 4-1 and Figures 4-3, 4-4, and 4-5, the first bit of code that looks unfamiliar should be the use of the columns property. This is shorthand to define values for two CSS properties (see Listing 4-2).

Listing 4-2. Defining the <article> with a class of multicol as Having Four Columns, Each of Width 12em

```
.multicol {
  columns: 4 12em;
}
```

As I just mentioned, the columns property is shorthand for two CSS properties: column-count and column-width. In this case, I've assigned the .multicol element to have four columns and a width of 12em for each column. It's important to note that the browser will not necessarily render exactly what you specify. If there's not enough space to create four columns, each 12em width, the rendering engine drops columns to make the columns fit. As a result, the width may not be 12em, and the number of columns may not be four!

This means when you're defining columns using the CSS Multi-column Layout module, you can't be certain that a browser will render exactly what you expect intuitively. This may sound like a bad bit of implementation; but as you'll see, it's the basis for one of the most powerful aspects of the module: CSS3 Multi-column Layout is responsive by default.

column-count

column-count defines the number of columns into which a multicol element should be divided. As you'll see, rules determine whether the browser respects this property. If it's unspecified or set to auto, the space is divided according to the column-width property value.

column-width

column-width specified the *minimum* width each column should occupy within the multicol element. Note that I said minimum, not definitive! Again, the rendering engine follows a series of logical rules to determine whether this rule is strictly adhered to. If it's unspecified or set to auto, the column width is determined by the number of columns it's split into—according to the column-count property value.

columns

The columns property is an effective shortcut for the combination of the column-count and column-width properties. Depending on the value(s) you pass into the columns property, the browser interprets your intentions differently, so it's important to understand all the possible permutations. I've borrowed the W3C's example code in code Listing 4-3 to help illustrate.

A simple way to remember how this works is that if you use a single value with a unit, the browser interprets this as a column-width value. If you omit a unit, the value is interpreted as a column-count value. If you're unsure, specify two values: one with a unit for width, and one without for count.

Listing 4-3. Effective Longhand Version of Each of Six Property Values Assigned Using the columns Shorthand Property

```
columns: 12em;       /* equates to column-width: 12em; column-count: auto */
columns: auto 12em;  /* equates to column-width: 12em; column-count: auto */
columns: 2;          /* equates to column-width: auto; column-count: 2 */
columns: 2 auto;     /* equates to column-width: auto; column-count: 2 */
columns: auto;       /* equates to column-width: auto; column-count: auto */
columns: auto auto;  /* equates to column-width: auto; column-count: auto */
```

The Rules for Dropping Columns and Changing Widths

As mentioned, the browser's rendering engine does not always adhere strictly to your definition of the width and total number of columns for a multicol element. The rules for how and when to alter the rendering intent are defined by the W3C's CSS3 Multi-column Layout module specification. The W3C offers a pseudocode listing to show the logic to be applied. I've copied this in Listing 4-4; you can find my translation of the rules after the listing, so don't worry about understanding this code!

Listing 4-4. W3C's Pseudocode for Calculating the Width and Number of Columns According to the Values Set for the column-width and column-count Properties

```
if ((column-width = auto) and (column-count = auto)) then
    exit; /* not a multicol element */

if ((available-width = unknown) and (column-count = auto)) then
    exit; /* no columns */
```

```
if (available-width = unknown) and (column-count != auto) and (column-width != auto) then
    N := column-count;
    W := column-width;
    exit;

if (available-width = unknown) then
    available-width := shrink-to-fit;

if (column-width = auto) and (column-count != auto) then
    N := column-count;
    W := max(0, (available-width - ((N - 1) * column-gap)) / N);
    exit;

if (column-width != auto) and (column-count = auto) then
    N := max(1, floor((available-width + column-gap) / (column-width + column-gap)));
    W := ((available-width + column-gap) / N) - column-gap;
    exit;

if (column-width != auto) and (column-count != auto) then
    N := min(column-count, floor((available-width + column-gap) / (column-width + column-gap)))
    W := ((available-width + column-gap) / N) - column-gap;
    Exit
```

Following is my translation of the pseudocode in Listing 4-4. Note that the rules and conditions are compared and acted on in order:

1. If the column-count and column-width properties are both either unset or set to auto, no columns are rendered. The same is true if column-count is set to auto and the width of the multicol element is unrestricted.

2. If the column-count and column-width properties both have values and a width hasn't been specified for the multicol element, use the values exactly as they are specified.

3. If the column-count property has been set with a value other than auto and the column-width property has been set to auto, divide the available width into the number of columns specified.

4. If the column-width property has been set with a value other than auto, the column-count property has been set to auto, and the container has a specified width, set the number of columns to match the available space divided by the specified width of each column. This may mean the columns end up wider than specified, if the width of the multicol element doesn't divide perfectly by the specified width of each column.

5. If the column-count and column-width properties have both been set with a value other than auto and the width of the multicol element has been set, look at whether the combination of width and count will fit inside the container element. If not, reduce the number of columns to match the number of times the specified width of each column will fit in the available space, and then expand the column width to fill the multicol element using the calculated column-count.

I hope you can see that this approach not only makes sense but also makes the CSS3 Multi-column Layout module very flexible. It's engineered to be responsive automatically while trying to honor the specified values for the `column-count` and `column-width` properties as closely as possible.

column-gap

If you were paying attention to the code in Listing 4-4, you'll have spotted a new property I haven't discussed yet: `column-gap`. `column-gap` is used to define the gutter width between columns. The example in Figure 4-3 uses `column-gap`. You can see the complete definition for the `.multicol` element again in Listing 4-5.

Listing 4-5. Stylesheet Definition for the `.multicol` Element, Showing the `column-gap` Property in Use

```
.multicol {
  position:    relative;
  margin:    auto;
  max-width:    960px;
  columns:    4 12em;
  column-gap:    2em;
  column-rule:    1px solid red;
}
```

Unlike the `column-width` and `column-count` properties, the `column-gap` property is absolute. This means if you specify a value, the browser will respect that setting, even if it means sacrificing columns.

column-rule

The `column-rule` property controls whether a dividing line is drawn between rendered columns. Column-rule works in much the same way as the `border` property from CSS 1 and 2.1. In fact, as with the `border` property, `column-rule` is a shorthand property for three different properties:

- Column-rule-width: As with `border-width`, this property takes an argument with a unit such as 2px, or the keyword none.

- Column-rule-style: Sets the line style to be rendered. The same options are available as with `border-style`, including dotted, dashed, solid, and so on.

- Column-rule-color: This color attribute can be set using any of the color models supported by the browser, including hex and rgb().

■ **Note**   A column rule is *always* drawn in the exact center of the column gap (gutter).

The column rule (see Figure 4-6) renders as if the column is completely filled with content, regardless of whether this is true. This is useful if your stylesheet definition calls for something other than a balanced fill to your columns, because it helps to visually define the space a column occupies, even if it's empty of content. Think back to how difficult it was to achieve this simple effect using floated elements to generate columns!

Figure 4-6. *The column rule in action*

Column Breaks

Normally, the browser's rendering engine decides how and where to break content across columns within a multicol element. This works well in many cases, but there may be times when you want to control the way content breaks. For example, you might want to force content to start rendering in a new column before each <h3> tag. Three properties are available to provide control over how and when to break content: break-before, break-after, and break-inside.

break-before

This property specifies that a break should be applied *before* the element it's applied to. It accepts the following values: auto | always | avoid | left | right | page | column | avoid-page | avoid-column. Of particular interest in the case of CSS3 Multi-column Layout are the column and avoid-column options, which ensure or prevent (where possible) a break in a multicol element.

break-after

This property specifies that a break should be applied *after* the element it's applied to. It accepts the following values: auto | always | avoid | left | right | page | column | avoid-page | avoid-column. Of particular interest in the case of CSS3 Multi-column Layout are the column and avoid-column options, which ensure or prevent (where possible) a break in a multicol element.

break-inside

Unlike the other two options, break-inside controls how content breaks inside the element it's applied to. It accepts the following values: auto | always | avoid | avoid-page | avoid-column. Of particular interest in the case of CSS3 Multi-column Layout are the column and avoid-column options, which ensure or prevent (where possible) a break in a multicol element.

■ **Note** Where a column break splits a box, that box's margin, border, and padding have no visual effect on where that split occurs. The margin immediately after the split is honored, however.

---

column-span

The column-span property allows a block-level element within a column to break outside the bounds of that column. In the future it may be possible to specify a number of columns to span, much like the colspan attribute that can be applied to a table cell, but in the CSS3 specification there are only two possible values: none and all.

By default, column-span is set to none. This means content renders within the constraints of the column. If it's set to all, the column is broken at the point that element is rendered. This creates an effect where a multicol element can contain multiple rows of columns.

Images, Responsiveness, and Cropping in Columns

Images present a special problem in a layout where you can't be absolutely certain how much space will be allocated to their display. There are two ways to approach images in a columnar layout:

- Fill the column width with an image, enlarging or reducing the image to match the available space.

- Predetermine the size at which an image should be shown, and wrap text around or crop the image as necessary to fill the space.

The example in Listing 4-1, shown in Figures 4-3, 4-4, and 4-5, uses the first option. Using a CSS rule of width 100% forces the image to render at the full column width. This effectively makes the image responsive, because it grows and shrinks to match the available space.

The alternative approach is to render an image at a set size. Just as with any other block-level container, floated elements work in a multicol element but are restricted to the space within the column in which they're rendered. Additionally, if an image is rendered so that it would occupy more horizontal space than is available in the column, the image is cropped at the edge of the effective content box for that column. The difference between these two different approaches to rendering images is shown in Figure 4-7.

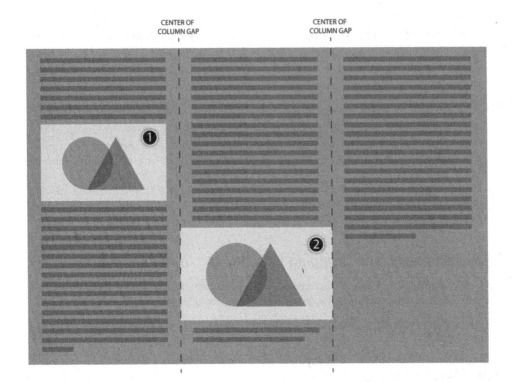

Figure 4-7. *Image 1 is set to 100% width, which allows it to scale to fit the column width. Image 2 uses an absolute size, forcing it to crop to the column width when the column is narrower than the image*

■ **Note** If you want your images to be responsive, use the first approach, because it enables images to resize according to the available space.

Controlling How Columns Are Filled with Content

Columns can be filled with content in two ways using CSS3 Multi-column Layout: they can either have content balanced across them or be filled sequentially until content runs out. If you use the latter option, there's a chance that one or more columns could be rendered without any content.

The `column-fill` property provides control over which approach the browser uses. It accepts two possible values: `balance` and `auto`. As you might expect, `balance` renders content equally across all available columns, and `auto` uses the sequential approach. The default (unspecified) value is `balance`, so if you don't explicitly set `column-fill` to `auto`, the browser attempts to render a balanced column fill. The code in Listing 4-6 and the in-browser result in Figure 4-8 show the same content rendered using the two options.

Listing 4-6. Two Different Column-Fill Approaches

```
<style>
 .multicol1 {
  columns: 3 20em;
  column-fill: balance;
 }
 .multicol2 {
  columns: 3 20em;
  column-fill: auto;
 }
</style>
<div class="multicol1">
 <p>Cras justo odio, dapibus ac facilisis in, egestas eget quam. Lorem ipsum dolor sit amet,
 consectetur adipiscing elit. Nullam quis risus eget urna mollis ornare vel eu leo. Nulla
 vitae elit libero, a pharetra augue. Sed posuere consectetur est at lobortis.</p>
 <p>....</p>
</div>
<div class="multicol2">
 <p>Cras justo odio, dapibus ac facilisis in, egestas eget quam. Lorem ipsum dolor sit amet,
 consectetur adipiscing elit. Nullam quis risus eget urna mollis ornare vel eu leo. Nulla
 vitae elit libero, a pharetra augue. Sed posuere consectetur est at lobortis.</p>
 <p>....</p>
</div>
```

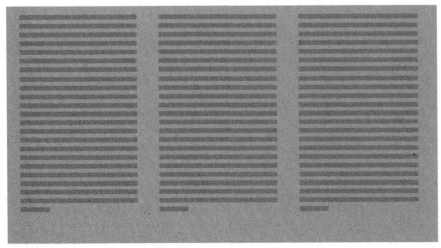

column-fill: balance

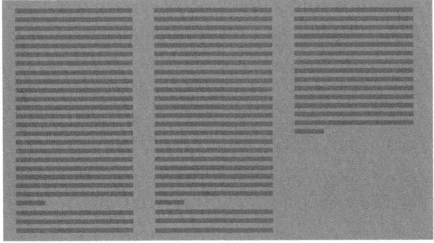

column-fill: auto

Figure 4-8. *The two different column-fill options. The first balances the content equally across the columns, and the latter fills columns sequentially*

Controlling How Column Content Overflows

As you've seen with images that extend beyond the bounds of a column, content that extends into the column gaps is clipped in the middle of the column gap. Have another look at the diagram in Figure 4-7 to see this in action.

When content extends beyond the space allocated for a multicol element, the browser can render this a few different ways depending on what settings you use in your CSS code. Sometimes this can result in additional columns being rendered outside the multicol block. The best way to understand this is by using two simple examples.

The code in Listing 4-7 creates a simple multicol element with three columns and fills it with content that includes forced column breaks after each paragraph. When you add a fourth paragraph to the HTML code, the browser continues to honor the forced breaks and creates a fourth column to accommodate the additional paragraph. This is rendered outside the content box for the multicol element because there is enough space to accommodate the three columns specified, and you explicitly declare a column width (see Figure 4-9).

Listing 4-7. Example of an Extra Column Rendering Outside the Content Box

```
<style>
 .multicol {
  width: 60em;
  columns: 3 18em;
 }
 p {
 break-after: column;
 }
</style>
<div class="multicol">
<p>Cras justo odio, dapibus ac facilisis in, egestas eget quam. Lorem ipsum dolor sit amet,
consectetur adipiscing elit. Nullam quis risus eget urna mollis ornare vel eu leo. Nulla
vitae elit libero, a pharetra augue. Sed posuere consectetur est at lobortis.</p>
<p>Donec id elit non mi porta gravida at eget metus. Etiam porta sem malesuada magna mollis
euismod. Cras justo odio, dapibus ac facilisis in, egestas eget quam. Aenean eu leo quam.
Pellentesque ornare sem lacinia quam venenatis vestibulum. Lorem ipsum dolor sit amet,
consectetur adipiscing elit.</p>
<p>Nulla vitae elit libero, a pharetra augue. Fusce dapibus, tellus ac cursus commodo,
tortor mauris condimentum nibh, ut fermentum massa justo sit amet risus. Vivamus sagittis
lacus vel augue laoreet rutrum faucibus dolor auctor. Curabitur blandit tempus porttitor.
Vivamus sagittis lacus vel augue laoreet rutrum faucibus dolor auctor. Fusce dapibus,
tellus ac cursus commodo, tortor mauris condimentum nibh, ut fermentum massa justo sit amet
risus. Vivamus sagittis lacus vel augue laoreet rutrum faucibus dolor auctor.</p>
<p>Maecenas sed diam eget risus varius blandit sit amet non magna. Vestibulum id ligula
porta felis euismod semper. Nullam quis risus eget urna mollis ornare vel eu leo. Cum
sociis natoque penatibus et magnis dis parturient montes, nascetur ridiculus mus. Donec
ullamcorper nulla non metus auctor fringilla. Fusce dapibus, tellus ac cursus commodo,
tortor mauris condimentum nibh, ut fermentum massa justo sit amet risus.</p>
</div>
```

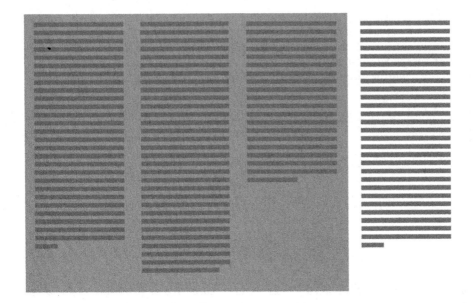

Figure 4-9. *If you force a break after the end of each paragraph, adding a fourth paragraph forces an additional column to render outside the content box*

In Figure 4-9, the content has been forced into an additional column in the inline direction. The same effect happens if a height is specified explicitly for the multicol element and the amount of content to be rendered exceeds the available space.

As with any block-level element, if you specify a value for the overflow property, it is honored, enabling control over whether additional columns are rendered in the document. The easiest way to avoid additional columns being generated is to not specify the height of the multicol element and to avoid forced column breaks.

There are also special rules for how paged media, such as a printed page, treat overflowing content. Read the W3C specification for full details.

How to Use CSS Multi-column Layout

As you can see, CSS Multi-column Layout provides a sensible and practical solution to the problem of arranging content into columns akin to a newspaper. Perhaps the biggest benefit of the module is the workflow improvements it brings to the web design process, making shims and workarounds a thing of the past. In addition, the module is responsive by default, offering a really useful option for a mobile-first design methodology, and also reducing the amount of development time required to achieve an effective solution across all screen resolutions.

CSS Multi-column Layout is a great overall layout tool, but it can also be used to create smaller in-page user interface elements such as these:

- Forms where content is arranged into columns on larger screens but falls back to a single column on mobile devices

- Horizontal navigation menus where it's important that every element occupies the same amount of horizontal space (although check out chapter 5 on Flexbox for an even better option for this purpose!)

- Rendering content in areas where you don't know in advance how much content or horizontal space you'll have available

That said, the primary purpose of CSS Multi-column Layout is as an overall page-layout tool, and this is where you'll get the maximum benefit from it.

Browser Support

Browser support for CSS Multi-column Layout is already very good. Every major browser has had support for at least two versions. Internet Explorer currently has the most complete implementation, with the current version offering full support, and partial support for the specification since version 10. Firefox, Chrome, Safari, and Opera all also feature working partial support for the specification, with the WebKit-based browsers offering full support. On mobile platforms, the picture is similar: all the common browsers have good support, with IE mobile offering the most complete implementation of all.

The CSS Multi-column Layout module reached Candidate Recommendation status in April 2011, which effectively means it's a complete module that you can consider stable. Despite this, work continues to be conducted by the CSSWG to refine and further develop the module. You can check the latest browser support for CSS Multi-column Layout at `http://caniuse.com/#feat=multicolumn`.

■ **Caution**   Although While browser support for this module is superb, older implementations of the standard may contain errors or bugs. As with any new module, to ensure best results, you must test in all possible browser configurations. Don't assume that every browser will render your `multicol` element identically.

Fallback Options and Polyfills

Browsers that don't understand CSS Multi-column Layout properties fall back to their default values for each element. This means in most cases that elements designed to have multiple columns render in a single column instead. For many layouts, this isn't much of an issue and is a reasonable outcome for a progressive enhancement approach to layout. If you absolutely must have columns in your layout, regardless of browser support for CSS Multi-column Layout, using the Modernizr framework will allow you to identify and handle browsers that can't render CSS columns. You can find out more at `http://modernizr.com`.

Real-world Example

Although multi-column layouts aren't anything new, the workflow improvements the new module brings are significant for web designers. As such, it's well worth exploring a real-world example to see how everything fits together. You're not going to be wowed by an entirely new visual paradigm, but if you've worked on the Web for any length of time, you'll appreciate the beauty in the code!

The Mockup

For this example, I've created a mockup of a page design for a fictional online newspaper. The rendered output is shown in Figure 4-10. This example uses the CSS Multi-column Layout module to render all the columns shown in the design, including the nested columns at the top of the layout where there are three callouts in a row. It also uses a number of the features discussed in this chapter, including the `column-span` property to create an effective pull-quote.

Figure 4-10. *A mockup for a fictional online newspaper*

The HTML Markup

The HTML markup for this page is very simple. At its core, there's a set of elements, each of which contains a single article. The markup works regardless of whether the user's browser supports CSS Multi-column Layout. Listing 4-8 shows the HTML code for the entire page.

Listing 4-8. HTML Code for the CSS Multi-column Layout Page

```
<div id="container">
 <header>
 <hgroup>
  <h1><span>the</span>news</h1>
  <h2>Your daily news</h2>
 </hgroup>
 <nav id="primarynav">
  <ul>
  <li>News</li>
   <li>Sport</li>
   <li>Culture</li>
   <li>The Arts</li>
   <li>Business</li>
   <li>Economy</li>
   <li>Lifestyle</li>
   <li>Travel</li>
   <li>Technology</li>
   <li>Comment</li>
  </ul>
 </nav>
 </header>
```

```
<section id="news">
<nav id="sectionnav">
<ul>
 <li>News</li>
 <li>US & Canada</li>
 <li>World</li>
 <li>Politics</li>
 <li>Media</li>
 <li>Education</li>
 <li>Science</li>
 <li>Entertainment</li>
 <li>Weather</li>
</ul>
</nav>
<div id="pagelayout">
<div id="mainlayout">
 <div id="callouts">
 <div class="callout1">
  <img src="images/callout1.jpg" />
  <h2>Banks in Recovery</h2>
 </div>
 <div class="callout2">
  <img src="images/callout2.jpg" />
  <h2>Weekend ideas</h2>
 </div>
 <div class="callout3">
  <img src="images/callout3.jpg" />
  <h2>New museum set to open</h2>
 </div>
</div> <!-- End Callouts -->
<article>
 <h2>Island boat service due to stop in September</h2>
 <figure>
  <img src="images/article.jpg" />
  <figcaption>Above: The service provides a lifeline to the local island community</figcaption>
 </figure>
<p>Etiam porta sem malesuada magna mollis euismod. Duis mollis, est non commodo luctus, ....</p>
<h3>Nullam id dolor id nibh ultricies vehicula ut id elit. Nullam id dolor id nibh ultricies
     vehicula ut id elit. Nullam id dolor id nibh ultricies vehicula ut id elit.</h3>
 <p>Etiam porta sem malesuada magna mollis euismod. Duis mollis, est non commodo luctus....</p>
 </article>
</div> <!-- End Main Layout -->
<aside>
 <div id="promoted">
  <article>
   <img src="images/promoted1.jpg" />
    <h3>Jobs of the future</h3>
    <p>Susan Hill explains why the jobs market our children will face bears no relation to
    today's workplace</p>
   </article>
```

```
    <article>
      <img src="images/promoted2.jpg" />
      <h3>10 amazing getaways</h3>
      <p>Our top pick of summer breaks on a budget, that offer a lot of bang for your bucks</p>
    </article>
  </div> <!-- End Promoted -->
  <div id="features">
    <h4>Features</h4>
    <ul>
      <li>
        <img src="images/featured1.jpg" />
        <h5>Rise of the cupcake</h5>
        <p>Inceptos Aenean Dolor Sit Commodo</p>
      </li>
      <li>...</li>
    </ul>
  </div> <!-- End Features -->
  </aside>
  </div> <!-- End Page Layout -->
  </section>
</div>
```

Rendering Columns

This layout is definitely achievable using only CSS2.1, but the new CSS Multi-column Layout module makes it much easier to maintain the content on the page without having to adjust markup or manually paginate the content. I'll show you each section in isolation so you can see just how useful the CSS Multi-column Layout module can be.

■ **Note**   As with many CSS3 properties, during the implementation phase, browser vendors added prefixes to the properties. I'm showing you code without the prefixes to keep the listings clean. Check with the browsers you're targeting to see whether you need to use vendor-prefixed versions of each property.

The Main Article

The main headline and article area follow a logical design pattern that's used throughout the book. The CSS is shown in Listing 4-9. This is all the code necessary to achieve the columnar layout shown in Figure 4-10.

Listing 4-9. CSS Code Used to Create the Main Article's Multi-column Layout

```
#mainlayout {
  max-width: 560px;
  columns: 2 250px;
  column-rule: 1px solid #999;
  column-gap: 20px;
}
```

```
#mainlayout article p {
  font-size: 1.1em;
  line-height: 1.7em;
}
#mainlayout article figure {
  width: 100%;
  margin: 0;
  padding: 0;
}
#mainlayout article figcaption {
  font-style: italic;
  font-size: 0.8em;
}
#mainlayout article figure img {
  width: 100%;
  border: 1px solid #297C21;
}
#mainlayout article h2 {
  color: #297C21;
  column-span: all;
  font-size: 2.2em;
  font-weight: normal;
}
#mainlayout article h3 {
  column-span:  all;
  padding: 10px 0px;
  border-top: 1px solid #999;
  border-bottom: 1px solid #999;
  font-weight: normal;
  color: #333;
  font-size: 1.5em;
  line-height: 1.5em;
}
```

The simple rules in this code create the layout necessary to render two columns in the main article area and break out of the column structure for a pullquote. The result is a set of columnar rows that render above and below the pullquote. Note that the code also uses column-span: all for the <h2> tag, which renders the headline across both columns. You can see the output in Figure 4-11, which is rendered in Safari.

Island boat service due to stop in September

Above: The service provides a lifeline to the local island community

Etiam porta sem malesuada magna mollis euismod. Duis mollis, est non commodo luctus, nisi erat porttitor ligula, eget lacinia odio sem nec elit. Donec id elit non mi porta gravida at eget metus. Donec ullamcorper nulla non metus auctor fringilla. Fusce dapibus, tellus ac cursus commodo, tortor mauris condimentum nibh, ut fermentum massa justo sit amet risus.

Nullam id dolor id nibh ultricies vehicula ut id elit. Nullam id dolor id nibh ultricies vehicula ut id elit. Nullam id dolor id nibh ultricies vehicula ut id elit.

Etiam porta sem malesuada magna mollis euismod. Duis mollis, est non commodo luctus, nisi erat porttitor ligula, eget lacinia odio sem nec elit. Donec id elit non mi porta gravida at eget metus. Donec ullamcorper nulla non metus auctor fringilla. Fusce dapibus, tellus ac cursus commodo, tortor mauris condimentum nibh, ut fermentum massa justo sit amet risus.

Etiam porta sem malesuada magna mollis euismod. Duis mollis, est non commodo luctus, nisi erat porttitor ligula, eget lacinia odio sem nec elit. Donec id elit non mi porta gravida at eget metus. Donec ullamcorper nulla non metus auctor fringilla. Fusce dapibus, tellus ac cursus commodo, tortor mauris condimentum nibh, ut fermentum massa justo sit amet risus.

Figure 4-11. *The primary article rendered in Safari*

Other Column Content

The other columns and content on the page are straightforward to render. Using the same principles, but slightly different values, you can render the top callout section. Because this callout area is a child of the main container, you first need to span both columns for the callout area and then set a `column-count` of 3 for the container, allowing the three callouts to render in three columns. The HTML is shown again in Listing 4-10, the relevant CSS in Listing 4-11, and the resultant render in Figure 4-12.

Listing 4-10. HTML for the Callout Area

```
<div id="mainlayout">
  <div id="callouts">
  <div class="callout1">
   <img src="images/callout1.jpg" />
   <h2>Banks in Recovery</h2>
  </div>
  <div class="callout2">
   <img src="images/callout2.jpg" />
   <h2>Weekend ideas</h2>
  </div>
```

```
<div class="callout3">
 <img src="images/callout3.jpg" />
 <h2>New museum set to open</h2>
 </div>
 </div> <!-- End Callouts -->
 ...
</div>
```

Listing 4-11. CSS Applied to the HTML in Listing 4-10, Spanning the #mainlayout Columns and Setting Up a Three-Column Layout for the Callout Area

```
#callouts {
 column-span: all;
 columns: 3 180px;
}
```

Figure 4-12. *The three-column callout area sitting above the two-column article, rendered in Safari*

The remaining bit of interest is the smaller column area to the right. This is rendered in a way similar to the main content area, but it includes stacking list items and features. The relevant HTML code is shown in Listing 4-12.

Listing 4-12. Sidebar Content Area

```
<aside>
 <div id="promoted">
  <article>
   <img src="images/promoted1.jpg" />
   <h3>Jobs of the future</h3>
   <p>Susan Hill explains why the jobs market our children will face bears no relation to
   today's workplace</p>
  </article>
```

```
<article>
 <img src="images/promoted2.jpg" />
 <h3>10 amazing getaways</h3>
 <p>Our top pick of summer breaks on a budget, that offer à lot of bang for your bucks</p>
</article>
</div> <!-- End Promoted -->
<div id="features">
 <h4>Features</h4>
 <ul>
  <li>
  <img src="images/featured1.jpg" />
  <h5>Rise of the cupcake</h5>
  <p>Inceptos Aenean Dolor Sit Commodo</p>
  </li>
  <li>...</li>
 </ul>
</div> <!-- End Features -->
</aside>
```

The CSS is actually very simple for this section of the page. The only CSS3 Multi-column Layout code required forces the second column into a new column and creates the two columns in the first place. The important bits are shown in Listing 4-13; the result appears in Figure 4-13.

Listing 4-13. Pertinent Bits of CSS Used to Achieve the Two-Column Layout in the Sidebar

```
#pagelayout > aside {
 max-width: 350px;
 columns: 2 160px;
 margin-left: 10px;
}
#pagelayout > aside img {
 width:  100%;
}
#features {
 break-before: column;
}
#features ul li img {
 clear: left;
 width: 35%;
 float: left;
}
```

Figure 4-13. *The resulting layout shows two columns in the sidebar area. Note that I've used a combination of image techniques in this layout, which is rendered in Safari*

Remember that CSS3 Multi-column Layout is responsive by default. This means as the available horizontal rendering space is reduced, so are the number of columns rendered in the main layout. Recall that you have a nested set of columns shown in the main article area. Because you haven't specified a maximum or fixed width for these columns, they shrink until they reach the minimum width of 220px. Once they hit that width, they can't get smaller; instead, the browser renders the content in a single column that expands to fill the available space. You can see this effect in Figure 4-14.

Figure 4-14. *Notice that when the browser window is pulled in to be narrower than a typical desktop resolution, the content automatically reformats to reduce the number of columns*

The same responsive reformatting happens when the content is viewed at smartphone resolution. You can simulate this effect by dragging the browser window to its smallest possible width. In this case, once the window is narrower than 500px, the content reformats again, displaying all the principal content in a single continuous column, as shown in Figure 4-15.

Figure 4-15. *On a smartphone, the page automatically responds, rendering content in a single column layout rather than in columns side by side*

■ **Note**   Some additional non-CSS-Multi-column-Layout CSS code is required to define the color, border, and typographic styles shown in Figures 4-10 through 4-15.

Summary

CSS Multi-column Layout offers an incredibly useful way to render content into reader-friendly columns that look good and are easy to maintain. This is the principle benefit of the new module, because it simplifies the creation of these complex layouts, making it significantly quicker to update content in the future and requiring substantially fewer hacks and workarounds to create the layout in the first place.

Browser support is extremely good, so this is one of the safest of all the new CSS3 layout modules to use on the Web. Non-supporting browsers automatically fall back to a single-column layout. And by using specified widths for individual columns, the layouts are also responsive by default, reformatting to fit smaller or larger screens automatically without any further code required.

With the use of a library such as Modernizr, it's easy to provide a polyfill set of styles using the older CSS 2.1 specification for non-compliant browsers. But in many cases this isn't strictly necessary, because most layouts suffer only marginally from a lack of columns to break up content.

CHAPTER 5

CSS Flexible Box Layout

The CSS Flexible Box Layout module solves a positioning problem that web designers have been struggling with since the first days of CSS: evenly spacing elements along a horizontal or vertical axis, without the need to resort to complicated floating or script-based hacks. This chapter goes into the Flexible Box Layout module in much more detail and shows how it can revolutionize the way you design your web pages.

■ **Note**   This module is commonly referred to as Flexbox, so throughout this chapter I use the terms Flexible Box Layout and Flexbox interchangeably to refer to the module.

What Is Flexbox?

CSS Flexible Box Layout provides a box model optimized for user interface design. Using the flex layout model, the child elements of a flex-enabled container can be laid out on an axis (either horizontal or vertical), and these child elements can automatically grow and shrink to fill the space available without overflowing the parent container. One particular benefit of the Flexbox module is the ease with which the alignment of child elements can be set and manipulated. This makes it simple to position content while retaining the flexibility to introduce additional sibling elements later: the days of using pixel-based layout are gone.

It's also possible to nest individual flex containers within other flex containers. This practice allows you to build layouts that are flexible across both axes by nesting a vertical container inside a horizontal container, or vice versa.

CSS 2.1 introduced and defined the four following layout modes for rendering web pages:

- *Block layout* for documents

- *Inline layout* for text

- *Table layout* for tabular data in a two-dimensional grid

- *Positioned layout* for explicitly positioning elements on the page, removing them from the document flow

The browser uses these systems when parsing CSS rules. These layout modes determine the size and position of elements based on their siblings, flow in the document, and parent elements.

© Sam Hampton-Smith 2016

S. Hampton-Smith, *Pro CSS3 Layout Techniques*, DOI 10.1007/978-1-4302-6503-0_5

Flexbox introduces a fifth layout mode that the W3C has named *flex layout* (see Figure 5-1). This mode is specifically designed for arranging complex user interface elements. Flex-layout mode considers the usage scenario of more complicated pages and web apps than CSS2.1 envisaged.

Figure 5-1. *Flexbox in action, rendering a page without the need to use workarounds to achieve the layout. You build this layout at the end of this chapter*

Syntax and Structure

The W3C CSSWG has been working on the Flexbox module since 2009, when the first working draft was published. During this time, the specification and syntax have changed substantially. The current specification includes a Candidate Recommendation, published in September 2012, and an Editor's Draft, which was updated in October 2013.

A Candidate Recommendation is considered to be stable, and this one forms the basis of the syntax detailed in this chapter. Although it's not dramatically different, the Editor's Draft introduces some refinements that I also cover. I'll point out where the syntax shown is derived from the Editor's Draft rather than the Candidate Recommendation. In addition, I'll let you know what support browsers currently offer.

■ **Note**   As of October 3, 2013, the latest version of the Flexbox module is an Editor's Draft, building on the W3C Candidate Recommendation. An Editor's Draft is open for discussion and can change over time. As a result, the syntax can't be considered stable. To avoid problems, ensure that you're working with the latest Candidate Recommendation. You can view the current Editor's Draft specification at `http://dev.w3.org/csswg/css-flexbox/`.

Basic Concepts and Terminology

In its introduction to Flexbox, the W3C describes flex layout as being superficially similar to block layout because they follow a similar design pattern. I find it helps to think of flex layout as being a bit like table layout, because of the way it allows elements to align and resize relative to the axis, much as a table's cells squash to fit in a row. As you'll see, flex layout is actually quite different, although it does share recognizable features from block, inline, and table layout.

At its core, flex layout is simple. But don't be fooled into thinking that Flexbox is less powerful because it's easy to pick up. It's an incredibly versatile layout module that allows you to perform the following tasks:

- Lay out elements in one of four different directions: left-to-right, right-to-left, top-to-bottom, or bottom-to-top

- Rearrange the order of elements solely using CSS

- Size elements to fit into the available space automatically

- Align elements according to the container or sibling elements, achieving common cross-axis proportions

- Collapse elements within the container without affecting the offset size of the container

- Create linear single-axis layouts or wrapped multiline layouts along the cross axis

Central to the flex layout mode is the idea of the axis. Flexbox is a two-dimensional layout tool, and there are two possible axes to work with: horizontal, which is referred to as row; and vertical, which is referred to as column.

A Flexbox layout requires an element to act as a *flex container* and zero or more child elements that are *flex items*. These flex items are laid out using the flex layout model, whereas the parent container can have other layout models applied to it (such as float). This means you can incorporate a flex container into your standard CSS 2.1 layout without having to change your entire structural approach.

Browser Support

Browser support for Flexible Box Layout is already very good. Internet Explorer has partially supported the specification since version 10, with full support included in IE11. Firefox, Chrome, Safari, and Opera all also feature at least partial support for the specification, with the WebKit-based browsers offering full support.

On mobile platforms, iOS Safari has good support, as does Blackberry's browser. IE mobile and Android's browser both have partial support. Only Opera Mini currently doesn't support the specification. You can check the latest browser support for Flexbox at http://caniuse.com/#search=flex.

■ **Caution**   During the development of the Flexible Box Layout module, some browsers implemented early versions of the specification. The syntax has since changed. As a result, many examples on the Web are now out of date, so be careful when following example code to ensure that you're using the correct version of the module.

Browsers that don't understand the Flexbox CSS properties fall back to their default values for each element. Typically, structural items such as <div>, <section>, and <article> display as block-level elements, whereas inline elements such as <span> revert to their default inline-level behavior. You can use this information to your advantage to handle older browsers; or, if you'd like to polyfill Flexbox-like rendering, the Modernizr JavaScript library allows you to test for browser support. You can find out more at http://modernizr.com.

Direction and Size

To fully understand what is meant by the direction of a Flexbox container's flow and where the start and end are, it helps to have common language defining the relative aspects of the Flexbox module. The W3C has made a good attempt at this in the Candidate Recommendation draft for Flexible Box Layout, so I use the same approach when talking about both direction and size.

The *main axis* of a flex container is the axis along which individual flex items are positioned. The *main start* and *main end* are defined according to the language of the page and align with the beginning and end of the *main size*. The *cross axis* runs perpendicular to the main axis and has a *cross start* and a *cross end*. Again, these are defined by the *cross size*.

Figure 5-2 demonstrates the different axes and naming conventions I use when discussing Flexbox. You'll probably want to refer back to this diagram until you feel comfortable with the concept of the two axes.

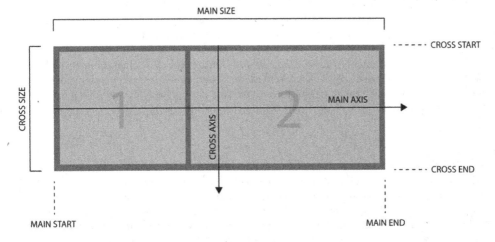

Figure 5-2. *Terms used when talking about Flexbox dimensions and flow direction*

An example will make this theory easier to understand. Listing 5-1 displays the code for this example. You can see the sample output in Figure 5-3. I explain what's going on in the following pages.

Listing 5-1. HTML Markup Being Styled with Flexbox CSS Properties

```
<section id=library">
 <article class="library-item">
  <h1>The Wonderful Wizard of Oz</h1>
  <h2>by L. Frank Baum</h2>
  <img src="images/oz.jpg" alt="Original cover of The Wonderful Wizard of Oz" />
  <button>Remove from library</button>
 </article>
```

```
<article class="library-item">
  <h1>Pride and Prejudice</h1>
  <h2>by Jane Austen</h2>
  <img src="images/pandp.jpg" alt="Pride and Prejudice book cover" />
  <button>Remove from library</button>
</article>
<article class="library-item">
  <h1>Adventures of Huckleberry Finn</h1>
  <h2>by Mark Twain</h2>
  <img src="images/huck.jpg" alt="Original cover of Huckleberry Finn" />
  <button>Remove from library</button>
</article>
</section>

<style>
#library {
  position: relative;
  display: flex;
  flex-flow: row wrap;
}
.library-item {
  display: flex;
  flex-flow: column;
}
.library-item > img {
  order: -1;
  align-self: center;
}
.library-item > button {
  margin-top: auto;
}
</style>
```

Figure 5-3. *The result of combining the HTML and CSS code shown in Listing 5-1*

■ **Note**   Some additional non-Flexbox code is required to define the color, border, and typographic styles shown in Figure 5-3.

Let's take a look at the different elements of this example.

The Flex Container

The *flex container* is the element inside which flex items are positioned according to the rules and properties of flex layout. *Flex items* are the direct children of a flex container. Each flex container can hold zero or more flex items, and these can either be explicit elements such as a <div>, <img>, <section>, and <article>, or a contiguous run of text, which is treated by Flexbox as if it were contained by an element.

You define an element as a flex container by using the display property, set to a value of either flex or inline-flex. The difference between display: flex and display: inline-flex is that display: flex defines the container as being a CSS 2.1 block-level item, whereas display: inline-flex sets the container to be an inline-level element. Listing 5-2 shows the code that defines the #library section as a flex container with its own flex context.

Listing 5-2. Defining the Library Element as a Flex Container by Assigning display: flex;

```
#library {
  display: flex;
}
```

When you define a flex container by using either display: flex or display: inline-flex, you're creating a new flex formatting context for the content of that container. This context only affects the flex item child elements of that container. External elements do not affect the nested flex items. The lack of awareness of external elements in the rendering of flex means float and clear have no effect on flex items. It's also worth noting that the column properties in the Multi-column Layout module have no effect on flex items.

The Flex Formatting Context

Each flex formatting context works independently of its counterparts in the layout. Therefore, Flexbox is not a good choice for creating a perfect grid, as you see later in this book when I discuss a module designed especially for the purpose of grid layout. This is because individual containers let their flex items expand or contract according to their size and content, without referring to flex items in an adjacent flex container. Grid-based layouts, in contrast, stick rigidly to a specified meter and rhythm that accounts for adjacent elements. Figure 5-4 illustrates three different flex containers, each with its own flex formatting context that pays no attention to the adjacent containers.

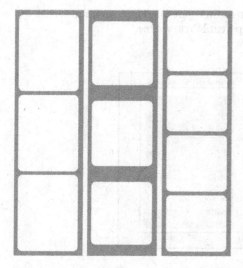

Figure 5-4. *Flex items are sized and positioned relative to their own flex container, not flex items inside other flex containers*

Display Models

Like the flex container, a flex item defines its own formatting context. This can be set using the display property and any of the CSS 2.1 permissible values. Consequently, you can set flex items to float, to display inline, or as a table-cell. If you use a display value of flex, the flex item itself becomes a flex container and supports additional properties such as visibility: collapse, which is discussed later in this chapter.

■ **Note**   If you use position: absolute or position: fixed, the flex item is taken out of the flex formatting context flow, unless both left and right or top and bottom are set with a value of auto. In this case, the values of these position properties are calculated from the flex item's static position in the context of the flex container.

In the next example, the primary flex container is a <section> element with an id of library. Each child—an <article> element with a class of library-item—is also set to use display: flex. Listing 5-3 isolates the relevant CSS.

Listing 5-3. CSS to Define Each Flex Item in the Context of the #library Flex Container

```
.library-item {
  display: flex;
  flex-flow: column;
}
```

Each of these flex items is in fact a flex container, as you can see in Figure 5-5. The contents of each item are thus also treated as flex items, but only in the context of the parent library-item.

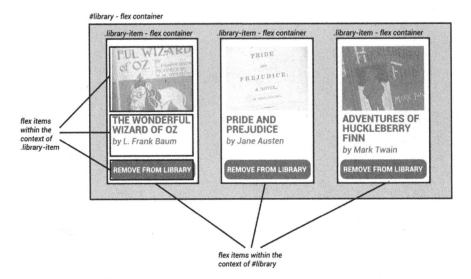

Figure 5-5. *Each flex item in the #library flex container acts as its own flex container, following a horizontal flex direction*

flex-direction

flex-direction is used to define the main axis for a flex container. Recall that Flexible Box Layout is a two-dimensional layout module, so there are only two axes to choose from:

- row: Horizontal in English.
- column: Vertical in English.

Each axis can run either forward or in reverse. The syntax for defining the reverse version of flex-direction: row is flex-direction: row-reverse; and for flex-direction: column, it's flex-direction: column-reverse.

■ **Caution** The terms row and column may make you think of horizontal and vertical layout, respectively, but in Flexbox this is only true for horizontal writing modes. In vertical languages, such as Japanese, row lays out content from top to bottom.

The default main axis, and thus flex-direction value, is set according to the writing mode being used on the web page. For English, this is left-to-right, top-to-bottom, defined as ltr. The result is that web pages created using the ltr writing mode default to row and run from left to right. Setting a value of row-reverse makes the flex items display from right to left.

flex-wrap

The flex-wrap property controls whether the flex container is single-line or multiline. There are three possible values:

- nowrap: Defines the flex container as being single-line. All the flex items in the container fit into one linear run without wrapping onto two or more lines. This is the default value for flex-wrap.

- wrap: Allows the flex items to be spread across two or more lines along the cross axis.

- wrap-reverse: Works like wrap, but runs in the opposite direction of the default.

If you allow your flex container to render across multiple lines by using a value of wrap or wrap-reverse, the flex items wrap into a second (or third, fourth, or fifth) line when there's not enough space to display all the items in a single line. This is a really useful option for responsive design, because it automatically repaginates the contents according to the container.

Just as with flex-direction, the default flex-wrap orientation is defined by the writing mode. For English, this is left-to-right, top-to-bottom. In some languages it may be right-to-left, top-to-bottom, or top-to-bottom, left-to-right. To avoid doubt, explicitly set the language and writing mode of your page using the lang and dir properties on your HTML element, as shown here:

```
<html lang="en" dir="ltr">
```

flex-flow

flex-flow provides a convenient short-hand for the flex-direction and flex-wrap properties. It allows you to use a single line to define both properties, but it can also be used without a value for flex-wrap, making it work just as flex-direction does. Listing 5-4 uses flex-flow, although because nowrap is the default value for flex-wrap, I could have omitted this second value. The resulting layout is shown on the left side of Figure 5-6; the right side shows what the layout would look like if I had specified wrap instead.

Listing 5-4. Flex-flow Shorthand Solution for Defining Both the flex-direction and flex-wrap Properties

```
.library-item {
 display: flex;
 flex-flow: column nowrap; /* nowrap is the default value for flex-wrap, so isn't strictly
 necessary here */
}
```

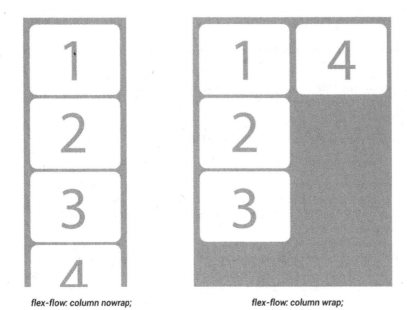

flex-flow: column nowrap;   flex-flow: column wrap;

Figure 5-6. *Notice the difference between the nowrap and wrap values for flow-wrap*

Controlling the Order of Items

One of the nicest features of Flexbox is the ability to control the order of flex items using pure CSS. This is a major step forward in allowing web designers to properly separate style from structure, and it brings benefits in search engine optimization, too.

By default, flex items are arranged along the main axis. By using the order property, you can override the default and specify the position of a particular item in the flow. Order takes an integer (whole number) value, with lower values rendering before higher values. Negative values are also allowed, as you can see in Listing 5-5.

Listing 5-5. Negative Value for the order Property, Forcing the Image to Render at the Beginning of the Flow Along the Main Axisy

```
.library-item > img {
 order: -1;
 align-self: center;
}
```

Let's change this CSS code to see the order property in action. Listing 5-6 shows the changes in bold. Figure 5-7 shows the result in order of the individual elements.

Listing 5-6. CSS Applied to the HTML Code in Listing 5-1, Updated to Include order Properties for the library-item Elements

```
<style>
#library {
  position: relative;
  display: flex;
  flex-flow: row wrap;
}
.library-item {
  display: flex;
  flex-flow: column;
}
.library-item:nth-child(1) {
  order: 3;
}
.library-item:nth-child(2) {
  order: 1;
}
.library-item:nth-child(3) {
  order: 2;
}
.library-item > img {
  order: -1;
  align-self: center;
}
.library-item > button {
  margin-top: auto;
}
</style>
```

Figure 5-7. By adding specific order property values to each library-item, you can reorder them along the main axis without having to change the markup

■ **Note**   The order property only affects visual media, so screen readers continue to read the content in the order it appears in the markup. It's important to understand this when checking the accessibility of your page layout.

Controlling the Flex

Perhaps the single most important part of the Flexbox specification is the ability to define how flex items are sized and spaced. Traditionally, it's been very difficult to arrange navigation items across an axis so that they expand or contract to fit the main size with equal spacing around them. Flexbox provides full control over both these design aspects through the following flex- properties:

- flex-grow
- flex-shrink
- flex-basis

The combination of these three properties enables fine control over whether an item grows to fill space or shrinks to fit when there's not enough space, and is the basis for the growing and shrinking. You see an example in a moment, but let's take a look at each property in turn first.

flex-grow

The flex-grow property defines how much the flex item grows, relative to the other flex items in the same flex container context. The value is specified as an integer and defaults to 1. Because this property is relative to the other items in the context, if you set a value of 2 for one specific item, any additional space is divided such that for every 10 pixels of additional space allocated to the other flex items, the item with a flex-grow value of 2 receives 20px of additional space. A value of 0 for the flex-grow property prevents any available additional space being given to the flex item.

flex-shrink

flex-shrink is similar to flex-grow but determines how space is allocated when flex items are shrinking to fit inside the flex container. Again, the value is an integer with a default of 1 and is relative to the other flex items in the container. A value of 0 for the flex-shrink property prevents the flex item from contracting when there is a lack of available space.

flex-basis

flex-basis sets the initial width for a flex item but can also be set to have a value of auto, which lets the browser calculate the width based on the contents of the item. When flex-basis is set to a positive value or auto, the basis for both flex-grow and flex-shrink is set to the spacing around the content. (See Figure 5-8.) When flex-basis is set with a value of 0, flex-shrink and flex-grow operate on the total space occupied by the item. (See Figure 5-9.)

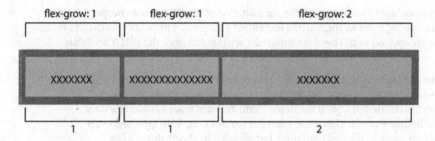

Figure 5-8. *When flex-basis is set with a value of 0, all the space is evenly distributed*

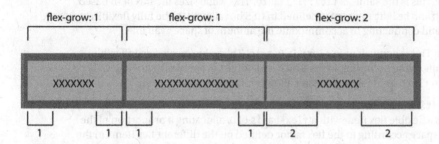

Figure 5-9. *When flex-basis is set with a value of auto or a width greater than 0, only the extra space is distributed*

The flex Shorthand Property and Its Special Cases

You can use the flex property as shorthand for flex-grow, flex-shrink, and flex-basis. There are some special rules about default values and omitted values for flex to account for the most common ways the W3C expects designers to use the property. These are shown in a moment for quick reference, but if you're in any doubt, be sure to specify each of the three values when using the flex property.

Listing 5-7 displays the syntax for the flex property. The property setting is equivalent to the individual properties shown after the listing.

Listing 5-7. flex-grow, flex-shrink, flex-basis, and the Shorthand flex Properties

```
// Syntax flex: <flex-grow> <flex-shrink> <flex-basis>
flex: 1 1 auto;
```

```
// This is short-hand for each of following property:value pairs
flex-grow: 1;
flex-shrink: 1;
flex-basis: auto;
```

There are several common usage scenarios for the combination of the three flex- properties, so the specification defines some special rules to apply when individual elements of the flex shorthand syntax are omitted or text values are applied to it. These are broken down directly from the W3C Candidate Recommendation:

- **flex: 0 auto** or **flex: initial**: This is equivalent to flex: 0 1 auto and is also the default value for the property. It sizes the flex item based on the width and height properties defined in CSS. If the item's main axis size is set to auto, the item is sized based on its contents. This value prevents the flex item from growing, even when there's free space in the flex container, but allows it to shrink down to its minimum size when there's inadequate space.

- **flex: auto**: This is the same as flex: 1 1 auto. This value sizes the flex item based on the width and height properties defined in CSS but allows it to be fully flexible, expanding and contracting to accommodate the amount of space available.

- **flex: none**: This is equivalent to flex: 0 0 auto. This value creates an inflexible flex item while sizing according to the width and height properties defined in CSS. It's similar to flex: initial but doesn't allow items to shrink.

- **flex: <positive-number>**: This is the same as flex: <positive-number> 1 0px. The result is a flexible flex item with a flex-basis of 0, allocating a proportion of the overall free space according to the flex factor defined on the different flex items in the container.

An Example of flex

The flex property provides one of the most exciting design opportunities of the entire Flexbox module. It's now trivial to create flexible layouts that are both responsive and proportional. Listing 5-8 illustrates this flexibility in action. (You see a more in-depth example at the end of this chapter.)

Listing 5-8. HTML Markup and CSS to Which the Flexbox Properties Are Being Applied

```
<style>
.layout {
 display: flex;
 flex-flow: row nowrap;
}
section > aside {
 flex: auto;
}
section > article {
 flex: 2 1 auto;
}
aside.level1 {
 order: -1;
}
aside.level2 {
 order: 2;
}
</style>
```

```
<section class="layout">
<article class="maincontent">
 ...
 </article>
 <aside class="level1">...</aside>
 <aside class="level2">...</aside>
</section>
```

The CSS applied to the markup in Listing 5-8 sets the main content <article> to occupy twice the space of the <aside> elements. All elements grow and shrink to fit the container, and the content is reordered to provide a typical three-column layout. This common layout approach is shown in diagram form in Figure 5-10; it would have required floating elements and a specific HTML order prior to Flexbox.

<section class="layout">

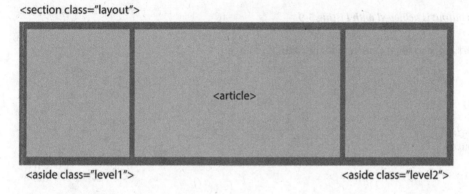

<aside class="level1">   <aside class="level2">

Figure 5-10. *The result of the combination of HTML code and CSS shown in Listing 5-8*

Controlling Alignment of Flex Items

The ability to expand and contract flex items and also align and size them along both the main axis and cross axis is one of the most useful aspects of Flexbox. For the first time with CSS, you can define accurately how items should align in the container and also determine the spacing between items. Although there have been script workarounds, it's been impossible to create a flexible, horizontally centered navigation bar until now. Even more impressive is the ability to align items vertically (or *cross axis*).

The Main Axis

There are two different ways to control alignment along the main axis in Flexbox: via the margin and justify-content properties.

Margin

Margins work on flex items in a very similar way to how CSS 2.1 margins operate on block-level elements. If you set an auto margin, any free space inside the flex container is assigned to that margin along that axis. So, by specifying `margin-left: auto` to a flex item, you push it to the right of the container (see Figure 5-11), whereas `margin-right: auto` pushes the item to the left. Using margin this way also prevents items from growing to fill the available space, because all the space is consumed by the margin. Listing 5-9 borrows an example from the W3C Candidate Recommendation specification to illustrate how margins can be used to push one list item to the right of a navigation bar.

Figure 5-11. *This output is achieved with Listing 5-9*

Listing 5-9. Using `margin` to Align One Item to the Main End Edge

```
<style>
 nav > ul {
  display: flex;
 }
 nav > ul > #login {
  margin-left: auto;
 }
</style>
<nav>
 <ul>
  <li><a href=/about>About</a>
  <li><a href=/projects>Projects</a>
  <li><a href=/interact>Interact</a>
  <li id='login'><a href=/login>Login</a>
 </ul>
</nav>
```

justify-content

Justify-content provides control over the type of alignment assigned to flex items in the flex container context along the main axis. The `justify-content` attribute is applied after any `margin` or `flex` has been calculated. It's most useful for layouts where a maximum flex item width has been specified or the items are in some way inflexible. Justify-content distributes the remaining available space.

There are five different possible values for `justify-content`:

- `flex-start` aligns items from the main start edge of the flex container. If your flex flow runs right to left horizontally, this means the flex items align to the left of the container.

- `flex-end` aligns items from the main end edge of the flex container. If your flex flow runs right to left horizontally, this means the flex items align to the right of the container.

- `center` is particularly exciting, because it allows items to be aligned to the center of the flex container, automatically taking into account the total main axis space occupied by all flex items and any spacing between them. This was impossible to achieve with CSS alone prior to Flexible Box Layout.

- `space-between` distributes flex items evenly across the main axis, with the first item aligning to the main start and the final item aligning to the main end edge. Note that if there's not enough space to accommodate all the flex items, this value behaves identically to `flex-start`.

- `space-around` is similar to `space-between` but adds a half-size space before the first item and after the last item. The remaining items are again distributed evenly between the first and last items.

Figure 5-12 illustrates these five options.

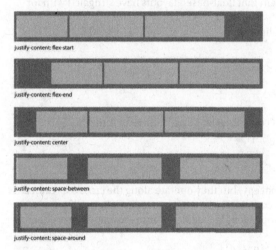

justify-content: flex-start

justify-content: flex-end

justify-content: center

justify-content: space-between

justify-content: space-around

Figure 5-12. *These alignment options are available with* `justify-content`

Working on Multiple Lines

One of the benefits of enabling a flex container to wrap onto multiple lines is the flexibility it brings to your layout. If you're using a Flexbox navigation bar, for example, you can allow individual navigation options to spill onto a second line if there are too many to fit on one line. This automatically makes your navigation bar responsive to different screen sizes.

As Figure 5-13 shows, the net result can be a little aesthetically unpleasant. As you've seen, however, you can use the `flex` attribute to cause the individual navigation items to pack the space. If you add a `flex: auto` rule to the flex items, the end result shown in Figure 5-14 is much prettier.

Figure 5-13. *A navigation bar with* `flex-wrap: wrap` *enabled*

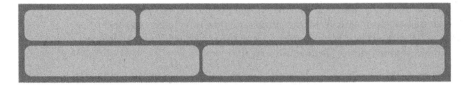

Figure 5-14. *The same navigation bar with* flex: auto *applied to the flex items*

Cross Axis Alignment

In addition to the ability to align along the main axis, Flexbox provides control over the alignment of flex items on the cross axis. Not only can you align, but you can also automatically stretch items so that they all occupy the same space on the cross axis, solving a problem that float-based layouts have struggled with for years.

Three properties are available to control cross axis alignment:

- align-items
- align-self
- align-content

Each of these properties exercises a different type of control, so let's look at them in turn.

align-items and align-self

align-items and align-self work similarly to justify-content, but they operate along the cross axis rather than the main axis. align-items is applicable to the flex container, whereas you can use align-self on individual flex items. As with justify-content, these properties are calculated after any margin has been applied.

These are the possible values for align-items and align-self:

- flex-start and flex-end work exactly as you might expect, aligning items either to the cross start or cross end edge, respectively.

- center aligns the items across the center of the cross axis based on the total dimension of the flex container along the cross axis. If the container is set to use a flex-flow value of wrap or wrap-reverse, allowing for multiple lines, the items are aligned along the center of the line within which they appear.

- baseline aligns the baselines of each item to the cross start edge.

- stretch expands the items along the cross axis to fill the line. This has the effect of making every flex item occupy the same space along the cross axis. If your flex items have a min-height/min-width or max-height/max-width set, these values still apply to the items, potentially resulting in items that either fail to fill the line or overflow the line. stretch is the default value for align-items.

- Auto is the default for align-self.

Figure 5-15 shows all the different options and the resulting layouts.

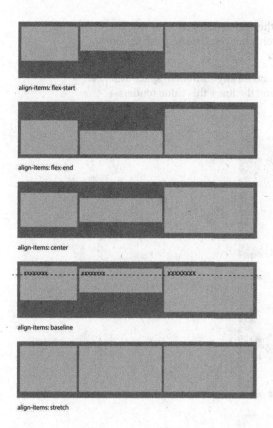

Figure 5-15. *These are the alignment options for* `align-items` *and* `align-self`

align-content

The align-content property works just like `justify-content` but acts on the lines within a `wrap` or `wrap-reverse` enabled flex container, determining how extra space is distributed across the lines. As with `justify-content`, there are several different possible values, which are shown in Figure 5-16:

- `flex-start` aligns lines from the cross start edge of the flex container. If your flex flow runs right to left horizontally, this means the lines align to the top of the container.

- `flex-end` aligns items from the cross end edge of the flex container. If your flex flow runs right to left horizontally, this means the lines align to the bottom of the container.

- `center` aligns all lines to the center of the flex container on the cross axis, automatically taking into account the total space occupied by all lines and any spacing between them.

- `space-between` distributes lines evenly along the cross axis, with the first line aligning to the cross start and the final line aligning to the cross end edge. Note that if there's not enough space to accommodate all the lines, this value behaves identically to `flex-start`.

- space-around adds a half-size space before the first line and after the last line. The remaining lines are again distributed evenly between the first and last lines. space-around is similar to justify-content.

- stretch causes lines to stretch automatically and fill any additional space available. If there's not enough space to accommodate all the lines, this value renders identically to flex-start.

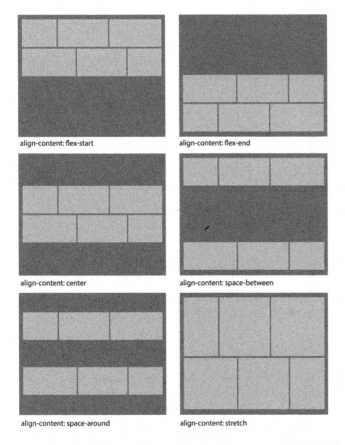

align-content: flex-start   align-content: flex-end

align-content: center   align-content: space-between

align-content: space-around   align-content: stretch

Figure 5-16. *Different align-content options are available for distributing and aligning individual lines in the flex container*

■ **Note**   align-content only works on flex containers with multiple lines. This is because a single-line container's line automatically fills the entire space allocated to the container.

Collapsed Items

You can collapse the visibility of flex items by specifying a value of collapse for the visibility property. This has the effect of removing the flex item from the render of a page while keeping it within the formatting structure. This allows collapsed items to define the overall proportion of a flex container's cross axis while being hidden from view.

This new option is particularly useful for user interface elements such as drop-down navigation menus, where only the top-level options are shown until the user selects an item and child items are shown. By continuing to affect the cross axis proportion, you can set menu sizes automatically according to the biggest option in the menu, even if this is collapsed. Listing 5-10 illustrates the behavior perfectly. Figure 5-17 displays the result.

Listing 5-10. Example from the W3C Specification, Showing a Dynamic Menu that Collapses the Visibility of Submenu Items

```
<style>
nav > ul > li {
  display: flex;
  flex-flow: column;
}
/* dynamically collapse submenus when not targeted */
nav > ul > li:not(:target):not(:hover) > ul {
  visibility: collapse;
}
</style>
<nav>
  <ul>
    <li id="nav-about"><a href="#nav-about">About</a>
    ...
    <li id="nav-projects"><a href="#nav-projects">Projects</a>
    <ul>
      <li><a href="...">Art</a>
      <li><a href="...">Architecture</a>
      <li><a href="...">Music</a>
    </ul>
    <li id="nav-interact"><a href="#nav-interact">Interact</a>
    ...
  </ul>
</nav>
```

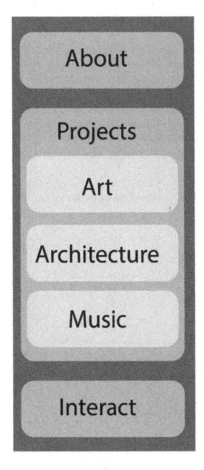

Figure 5-17. *The navigation menu with the second option opened to reveal the submenu. The widest submenu item sets the width of the overall menu container, despite being initially hidden*

How to Use Flexible Box Layout

By now you should have a clear idea of just how powerful and useful Flexbox is. It can singlehandedly solve many common layout issues, so it's tempting to think of Flexbox as the answer to all your layout needs. I want to discourage you from succumbing to this temptation. Although Flexible Box Layout is capable of rendering entire page layouts, other layout modules are designed more specifically for whole-page layouts (see the chapters before and after this one for some great options!).

Flexbox is better suited to individual user interface elements than overall page layout. Some common usage scenarios include the following:

- Elements you want to have true centering on both axes

- Scenarios where you have an unknown number of items to render, such as a menu controlled via a content management system

- Areas of a page where you want to reorder content from the markup order (although some of the other layout modules also allow you to do this)

- Tabs and groups of content where you're hiding content that isn't currently selected

- Forms and form element layout

Of course, there's nothing to stop you from using Flexbox as your primary layout tool, but it's worth considering the most appropriate layout module for the task at hand.

I couldn't let a chapter about Flexbox go without providing a real-world example of Flexbox in action. The following example is just one possible usage scenario that incorporates many of the properties you've seen in the preceding pages. If you weren't already convinced of the power and flexibility of the Flexible Box Layout module, I'm pretty sure this example will win you over.

Real-World Example

This example creates a mockup of a page design for a fictional real-estate company, shown in Figure 5-18. The example uses Flexbox to render several of the layout sections.

Figure 5-18. *A mockup for a fictional real-estate company*

The HTML Markup

The HTML markup that this page needs is basic. It follows a pattern similar to the layout designers have used in the past when using floats to arrange design elements. You could use Flexbox to create the entire page, but because it's better to use each module for its intended purpose, this example focuses on the following sections of the page:

- Navigation bar

- Jumbotron area

- Benefit statements

Listing 5-11 shows the relevant HTML code for these sections of the page.

Listing 5-11. HTML Code for Three Parts of the Page Suited to Flexbox Layout

```
<!-The navigation section -->
<nav>
 <ul>
  <li><a href="#">Home</a></li>
  <li><a href="#">Locations</a></li>
  <li><a href="#">Financing</a></li>
  <li><a href="#">Special Offers</a></li>
  <li><a href="#">About us</a></li>
  <li><a href="#">Contact Us</a></li>
  <li class="searchform"><form><input type="text" value="search" /></form></li>
 </ul>
</nav>

<!-The big icons/jumbotron section -->
<section id="jumbotron">
 <article>
  <h2>Free Advice</h2>
  <p>All our impartial advice is offered completely free of charge</p>
  <img src="images/bigicon-freeadvice.png" />
 </article>
 <article>
  <h2>Discounted Removals</h2>
  <p>Once you've found your dream...
...</article>
</section>

<!-The badge benefits section -->
<section id="benefits">
 <article>
  <h1> Looking for a beautiful new home that won't break the bank?</h1>
  <p> Nulla vitae elit libero, a pharetra augue. Nulla vitae elit libero, a pharetra augue.
  Cras mattis consectetur purus sit amet fermentum.</p>
 </article>
```

```
<article class="badge">
  <div>
  <h3>Quality without compromise</h3>
  <p>We have homes that suit every budget without compromising on quality</p>
  </div>
  <img src="images/badge-quality.png" />
</article>
<article class="badge">...
...</article>
</section>
```

Although this layout would be possible using CSS2.1, with Flexbox it becomes almost trivial to arrange the items correctly on the page. Let's look at each section in isolation so you can see just how powerful layout with Flexbox can be.

___

■ **Note** As with many CSS3 properties, during the implementation phase, browser vendors add prefixes to the properties. I'm showing you code without the prefixes to keep the listings clean. Until support is complete, you need to use vendor-prefixed versions of each property to fully support every browser.

___

Navigation

The navigation area follows the same design pattern you saw in Listing 5-9, so the code for this section is almost identical. Listing 5-12 shows all the code necessary to achieve the navigation layout shown in the mockup!

Listing 5-12. Flexbox CSS Code to Create the Navigation Layout

```
/* The navigation section */
nav > ul {
  display: flex;
  flex-flow: row wrap;
}
  nav > ul > .searchform {
  margin-left: auto;
}
```

The two simple rules in this code create the layout necessary to push the search form to the right of the navigation area. You can see the output in Figure 5-19, which is rendered in Chrome 30.

Figure 5-19. The navigation output in Chrome

The Jumbotron

The jumbotron area (with the big icons) is also simple to get into shape. Flexbox can help with several things that are going on in this area, such as the following:

- Each <article> is evenly sized.

- The content of each element in the jumbotron is aligned centrally on both axes.

- The image renders before the text but appears after the text in the markup.

In order to reorder this content, you would need to render each article as a flex container within the overall flex container, with an id of #jumbotron. See Listing 5-13.

Listing 5-13. Flexbox Code to Style the Jumbotron Section

```
/* The jumbotron section */
#jumbotron {
  display: flex;
  flex-flow: row wrap;
  align-content: stretch;
  justify-content: center;
}
#jumobtron article {
  display: flex;
  flex-flow: column nowrap;
  flex: 1 1 250px;
  align-content: center;
  justify-content: center;
}
#jumbotron article * {
  align-self: center;
}
#jumbotron article img {
  order: -1;
  flex: none;
}
```

Figure 5-20 shows the result, rendered in Chrome. Notice the base width of 250px for the flex of the <article> elements. This ensures that all the <article>s start at the same width and flex uniformly. It also means when a 960px window is used, three of the articles will fit horizontally into each row.

Figure 5-20. *When the window is wider than 960px, three* `<article>`*s render per row*

What happens when the window size is collapsed or the page is viewed on a mobile device? One of the major benefits of Flexbox is that it can be used as a responsive design tool. This code is flexible enough to deal with different window sizes. When the window gets a little narrower, the content repaginates so that only two `<article>`s appear per line, as you can see in Figure 5-21.

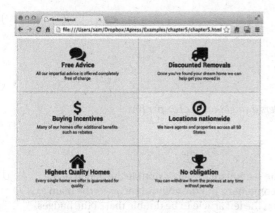

Figure 5-21. *When the window narrows, the content automatically reformats onto more lines*

The same thing happens when the content is viewed at smartphone resolution. You can simulate this effect by dragging the browser window to its smallest possible width. In this case, once the window is narrower than 500px, the content reformats again, displaying a single `<article>` per line (see Figure 5-22).

Figure 5-22. *At smartphone resolutions the content renders a single* `<article>` *per line*

The Benefits Area

The benefits area is a little more complicated, because the section on the left is double the height of the individual badge areas. This layout contains nested flex containers, but the column serves as the main axis instead of the row. This makes it possible to set the flex on the left article to be double that of the badges. See Listing 5-14 and the output in Chrome in Figure 5-23.

Listing 5-14. CSS Code for the Benefits Area

```
/* The badge benefits section */
#benefits {
 display: flex;
 flex-flow: column wrap;
 height: 260px;
}
#benefits article {
 flex: 2 2 260px;
 width: 318px;
}
```

```
#benefits article.badge {
  display: flex;
  flex-flow: row nowrap;
  flex: 1 1 130px;
}
#benefits article.badge img {
  order: -1;
  flex: none;
}
```

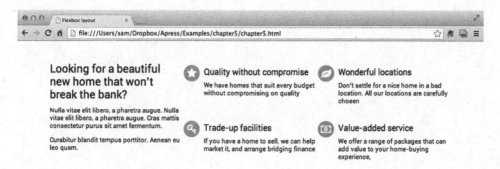

Figure 5-23. *The output in Chrome*

Notice that the article is set to use `flex: 2 2 260px`, and `article.badge` uses `flex: 1 1 130px`. The second rule overrides the first and forces all the badges to size uniformly. The remaining article is exactly double the height of the badges and has a `flex-grow` and `flex-shrink` value of 2, versus the badge values of 1. This enables `<article>` to occupy twice the height of the badges.

■ **Note** Some additional non-Flexbox CSS code is required to define the color, border, and typographic styles shown in Figures 5-18 through 5-23.

Summary

CSS Flexible Box Layout offers an extremely versatile layout model that is perfect for creating responsive user interface elements. The module uses an axis-based paradigm, and its contents can flex along the axis according to some simple rules defined through the `flex-` set of properties.

Flexbox solves many of the layout issues that have required elaborate workarounds up to this point. Arranging multiple items centrally in a container is now trivial, as is aligning and sizing boxes to match each other.

Browser support is largely good, so it's reasonably safe to use Flexbox on the Web. Non-supporting browsers automatically fall back to block-level layout in most cases. You can use a library such as Modernizr, which makes it easy to provide a polyfill set of styles using the older CSS 2.1 specification for these browsers.

CHAPTER 6

CSS Grid Layout

CSS Grid Layout provides a sensible solution to a standard layout paradigm that has been challenging web designers since the move away from table-based layout and the adoption of CSS for layout.

Note CSS Grid Layout is perhaps the most difficult of the new modules to use because browser support is still being developed. At the time of writing, the only render-reliable vendor is Microsoft, although by the time you are reading this book, this will likely have changed.

What Is CSS Grid Layout?

The W3C describes the CSS Grid Layout module as defining a two-dimensional layout system, optimized for user interface design. Crucially, and most usefully for layout designers, they go on to clarify that "In the grid layout model, the children of a grid container can be positioned into arbitrary slots in a flexible or fixed predefined layout grid." I talk about what this means in the coming pages, but it's good news!

Before I get to the technical aspects, it is worth reflecting on the use of a grid in layout design. You are already familiar with grid systems because you encounter them on a daily basis. Books and magazines use a grid system to create their layout so that elements on the page seem to have some relationship to one another. And every data table you have ever seen uses the exact same principles to help ensure that data points are correctly attributed to their legend. Indeed, it can be argued that grid-based layout was the first major design step the Web took: HTML <table> elements were used for layout rather than the display of data.

Unlike tables, however, grids should be able to display content with a layout-based bias rather than a data bias, and that is exactly what the CSS Grid Layout specification sets out to achieve. In some ways you can think of it in terms similar to CSS Flexbox; but instead of everything happening across just one axis, with CSS Grid Layout you use two dimensions: *block* and *inline* (or, if you prefer, *columns* and *rows*).

When used for layout, CSS Grid Layout is a really exciting module that makes it trivial to achieve flexible and fluid layouts that retain a prescribed relationship between elements on the page. This is in sharp contrast to the sometimes unpredictable and counterintuitive behavior you may encounter when using floating elements or tables, especially concerning compressed device or window widths. Figure 6-1 shows a typical usage scenario for a grid layout.

S. Hampton-Smith, *Pro CSS3 Layout Techniques*, DOI 10.1007/978-1-4302-6503-0_6

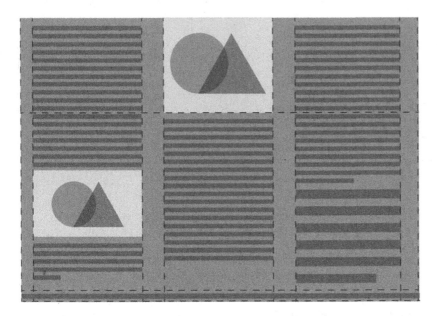

Figure 6-1. *A grid-based layout in action*

Grid Layout on the Web

The W3C CSSWG has been working on the CSS Grid Layout module since 2012, when the first working draft was published. During this time, the specification and syntax have changed substantially. The current specification at the time of writing was published in September 2015, and the syntax discussed here is based on the document found at www.w3.org/TR/css-grid-1/.

Be sure to check whether there is a more recent version of the specification at the time you are reading. Although the overall syntax is moving (slowly) toward stability, it is likely that there will be some changes to the syntax and structure of the module.

Just to reiterate, the specification is currently considered a working draft, which means there are a few stages to go before everything is set in stone for the 1.0 version of CSS3 Grid Layout. You are in the web design Wild West here, so strap on your cowboy boots!

■ **Note**　It is crucial that you understand that CSS Grid Layout is still in development. You can view the current working draft specification at www.w3.org/TR/css-grid-1/.

Why Use a Grid?

In order to make sense of why you might choose a grid system for your layout, it helps to have a picture in your mind of what a grid might look like. The W3C uses a pair of scenarios that I am borrowing here to help illustrate the ideas and concepts behind grids on the Web.

I have already talked about an inherent familiarity with grids as a layout tool for designers, but it is useful to understand that the tools of the Web have not offered any purposeful solution to creating a grid-based layout—until CSS Grid Layout! Designers historically used a combination of tables, scripts, and pixel-perfect floated elements to construct a layout with the appearance of a grid system. This worked well for fixed-width layouts where the designer could control or dictate the minimum viewport width. Those days are now gone, however, with the arrival of smartphones, tablets, and other web-connected devices. Layouts need to be able to adapt to a wide variety of device profiles and screen orientations.

The Basis of a Grid Layout

CSS Grid Layout is designed specifically to address this problem. At its basis, it allows you to divide the available space into a series of areas, each of which can be used for layout. Specific bits of content can then be positioned and sized to occupy individual columns, rows, and cells within this grid. Figure 6-2 is borrowed from the W3C's example layout to show a sbasic layout that might be created with CSS Grid Layout.

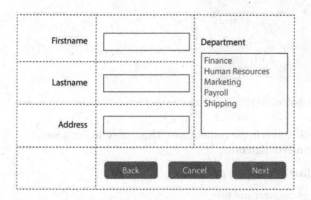

Figure 6-2. *A typical application layout that could be achieved with CSS Grid Layout*

Built-in Flexibility

One of the core principles behind CSS Grid Layout is that resizing layouts to fit the available space should not require additional work. Responsive design benefits are standard with CSS Grid Layout! Let's look at the example the W3C uses to explain this concept. (Thereafter I firmly move on to fresh examples!)

CSS Grid Layout is designed to work *responsively*. This means as the available viewport space is defined, elements intelligently reflow within the page. Figure 6-3 shows my interpretation of the W3C's example: a game screen with five different elements in the layout.

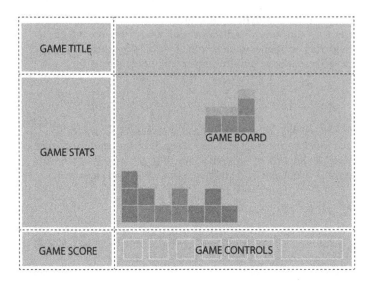

Figure 6-3. *My interpretation of the game screen used in the W3C's example project*

Note the dotted lines in Figure 6-3 that show divisions in the content area. These are grid lines! Some basic goals for the layout are specified in the imagined design brief:

- The stats area always appears immediately under the game title.

- The game board appears to the right of the stats and title.

- The top of the game title and the game board should always align.

- The bottom of the game board and the stats area align when the game has reached its minimum height, but otherwise the game board stretches to take advantage of all the screen real estate available to it.

- The score area should align into the column created by the game and stats area, and the controls are centered under the board.

Traditionally, this sort of layout might have used a combination of absolutely positioned elements with a specified width and height, floated elements and inline. The resulting code would be difficult to decipher and easy to break. Worse still, it would typically be unreliable across different resolutions.

By using CSS Grid Layout, you can achieve all of the brief's requirements! You look in detail at the properties and syntax in the next section; but first check out Figure 6-4, which shows the same diagram as Figure 6-3, but with the addition of width in the viewport. Listing 6-1 shows one way this layout can be achieved using CSS Grid Layout. (Don't worry too much about how the syntax works yet.)

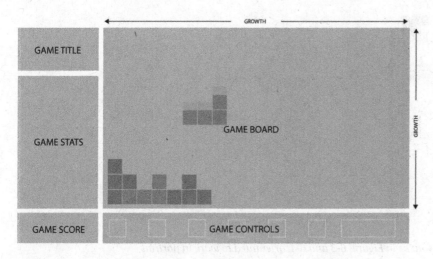

Figure 6-4. *The same layout you saw in Figure 6-3, but with additional width and height, allowing the board to grow*

Listing 6-1. Achieving the Layout Shown in Figures 6-3 and 6-4 Using CSS Grid Layout

```
<style>
#grid {
 display: grid;
 grid-template-columns: auto minmax(min-content, 1fr);
 grid-template-rows: auto minmax(min-content, 1fr) auto
}

#title { grid-column: 1; grid-row: 1 }
#score { grid-column: 1; grid-row: 3 }
#stats { grid-column: 1; grid-row: 2; align-self: start }
#board { grid-column: 2; grid-row: 1 / span 2; }
#controls { grid-column: 2; grid-row: 3; justify-self: center }
</style>

<div id="grid">
 <div id="title">Game Title</div>
 <div id="score">Score</div>
 <div id="stats">Stats</div>
 <div id="board">Board</div>
 <div id="controls">Controls</div>
</div>
```

Note that with some additional styling, the design can repaginate to suit portrait screens, as shown in Figure 6-5. You see how to use @media queries later in this chapter to achieve this level of responsiveness.

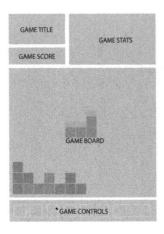

Figure 6-5. *The same layout as in Figures 6-3 and 6-4, orientated to work in portrait*

■ **Note**   There are many ways to achieve this layout using the CSS Grid Layout specification. This example is taken from the working draft at www.w3.org/TR/css-grid-1/ to illustrate the power of grids more than to suggest best practice.

Understanding the Terminology

I hope your appetite is whetted. Let's get on with the nitty gritty of how this module works. As with each CSS module, there are terms and language that are peculiar to CSS Grid Layout. It is partially defined by the W3C, but much of it has grown out of traditional graphic design and discussion about grid systems.

Any element that has a grid layout applied to it is referred to as a *grid container*. The *grid* itself is an intersecting group of horizontal and vertical lines that divide the grid container's space into a series of *rows* and *columns*. There are, therefore, two types of lines: one set that defines the columns that run along the *block axis* (also known as the *column axis*) and another set that runs orthogonally along the *inline axis* (also known as the *row axis*).

The terms *block* and *inline* directly refer to the CSS3 Writing Modes module, which means the column axis is not necessarily vertical top to bottom and the row axis is not necessarily horizontal left to right. For most work in the Latin-based languages, however, this is the principal experience of columns and rows; so for the purposes of understanding how the module works, it's OK to think in those terms. Figure 6-6 shows an illustration of the terms just defined.

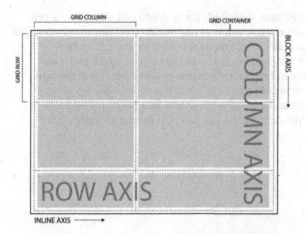

Figure 6-6. *The key terms used when describing grids in context*

You need to know some additional technical language before you can start exploring the properties that define and use CSS Grid Layout. A *grid track* is used to define either a grid column or a grid row. This is similar to the language used by CSS Flexbox, so if you have already read Chapter 5, it should sound familiar.

A *grid cell* is the space between two adjacent sets of grid lines on each axis. A grid cell is an area into which you can place content and is the smallest unit in the grid. Again, this is best illustrated with a diagram, so look at Figure 6-7, which shows the terms in context.

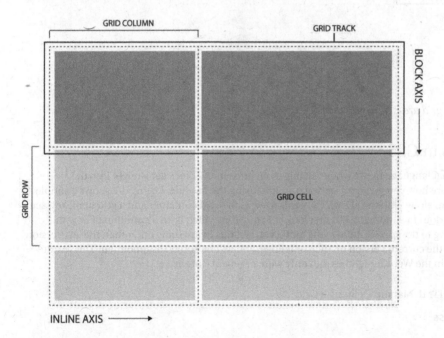

Figure 6-7. *The terms grid track and grid cell in context*

Let's not forget about the *grid lines*. These are the lines that divide the grid into *grid areas*, and as you have seen, you can describe them in terms of the axis along which they run. In CSS Grid Layout, you can also refer to individual lines explicitly using a numerical index or by a name specified in your CSS code.

Grid items are the individual elements that are assigned to a *grid area* (or *grid cell*) in the grid. *Grid areas* are defined by four *grid lines* in two pairs and can span more than one grid cell. Every grid container incorporates zero or more *grid items*; every child element of a *grid container* is automatically a *grid item*.

Figure 6-8 shows *grid lines*, *grid areas*, *grid cells*, and *grid items* in context. You will be pleased to hear that this is the last of the grid-related terminology you need before you can start getting dirty with code!

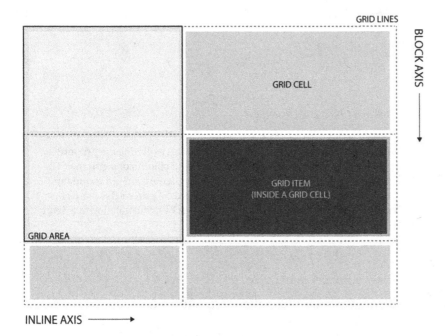

Figure 6-8. *Grid lines, grid areas, and grid items*

Defining Grids in CSS

Now that you know what language to use when talking about grids in CSS; let's get straight into the specification and explore how you go about setting up a grid using the module. Listing 6-2 shows a simple grid definition in action, along with the HTML elements used as the grid container and a grid item. You see what each line of code does in a moment, but first look at Figure 6-9, which is an illustration of how this should render according to the specification. Note that if you test this in anything other than the last version of Internet Explorer or the current version of Microsoft Edge, you will be sorely disappointed! This feature has recently appeared in the WebKit nightlies, but only with a -webkit- prefix.

Listing 6-2. CSS and HTML Markup Defining a Grid

```
<style type="text/css">
#gridcontainer {
display: grid;
grid-template-columns: 150px 1fr; /* two columns */
grid-template-rows: 50px 1fr 50px; /* three rows */
}
```

```
#griditem {
  grid-column: 2;
  grid-row-start: 1;
  grid-row-end: 4;
}
</style>

<div id="gridcontainer">
  <!-- begin the grid item -->
  <div id="griditem">
  <p>Some content or other...</p>
  </div>
  <!-- end the grid item -->
</div>
```

Figure 6-9 shows how this looks when rendered in the browser (or at least my illustration of how it should look). I added some extra shading to make the rows clearer.

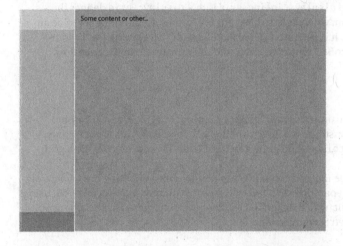

Figure 6-9. *An illustration of how the code shown in Listing 6-2 should render in the browser*

■ **Note** Some additional non-grid code is required to define the color, border, and typographic styles shown in Figure 6-9.

Let's look at the different elements of this example.

The Grid Container

The grid container is the element inside which grid items are positioned according to the rules and properties of the grid layout. You define an element as a grid container by using the display property, set to a value of either grid or inline-grid. Listing 6-3 highlights the code used to define the grid container.

Listing 6-3. Defining the gridcontainer Element as Being a Grid Container by Assigning display: grid;

```
#gridcontainer {
  display: grid;
}
```

When you define a grid container by using either display: grid or display: inline-grid, you create a new grid-formatting context for the contents of that container. This context only affects the grid item child elements of that container. External elements do not affect the nested grid items.

The Two Display Options for a Grid Container

The difference between display: grid and display: inline-grid is that display: grid defines the container as being a CSS 2.1 block-level item, whereas display: inline-grid sets the container to be an inline-level element. If this sounds familiar, it is because you are familiar with CSS Flexible Box Layout, which uses a similar approach and syntax concerning containers and their treatment in the page flow.

Defining Rows and Columns

When an element is made a grid container using display: grid or display: inline-grid, it has, by default, one column and one row, which constitute the full size of the grid container. This is not terribly useful, so you can use the grid-template-columns and grid-template-rows properties to divide a grid container into columns and rows.

In Listing 6-4, you can see how to divide the grid container into two columns and three rows. Each row or column is defined in turn, with a space separating each row or column definition. Values can be set using any measurement unit, including the fr unit, which defines a flexible space determined by the amount of space left after the fixed-size items have been accounted for.

Listing 6-4. Defining the Number of Rows and Columns in the Grid, Along with Their Proportions

```
#gridcontainer {
  display: grid;
  grid-template-columns: 150px 1fr; /* two columns */
  grid-template-rows: 50px 1fr 50px; /* three rows */
}
```

This defines two columns. The first is set to always occupy 150 pixels of space in the inline axis, and the second is allowed to fill the remaining space available in this axis.

Three rows are defined. The first and last are both set to occupy 50 pixels of space in the block axis. The middle row is set to fill the remaining space available in this axis. This means you have effectively created a fluid layout that always has a 150px × 50px cell at the beginning of the first column, followed by a fluid cell and then another fixed size cell. The second column is divided into three cells once again, but each is fluid on the inline axis, with the middle cell being fluid in both axes. Figure 6-10 illustrates this a little more clearly.

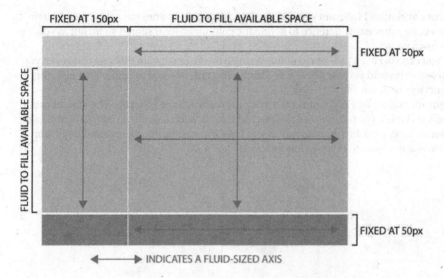

Figure 6-10. *The effect of the CSS definition of rows and columns in Listing 6-4; incorporating both fixed and fluid sizing*

■ **Note** The `fr` unit represents a fraction of the available free space, but because the example uses `fr` once in each axis, it equates to all the free space available.

THE FLEXIBLE-LENGTH FR UNIT

It is worth taking a moment to talk about the `fr` unit. The `fr` (or `<flex>`) unit is defined as a fraction of the available space. Each column's or row's share of the free space can be computed as the column's or row's `<flex>` * `<free space>` / `<sum of all flex factors>`. That is according to the W3C.

It is easiest to think in terms of adding all the fr units you use along one axis and then dividing the amount of free space to be allocated among elements using these units. So you could have one element with `3fr` taking up three times the amount of space that a sibling with `1fr` unit is assigned. If only those two elements were defined with the `fr` unit along that axis, the total available space would be calculated as being split into four, with three equal parts being assigned to the first element and the remaining equal part being assigned to the second.

Positioning Grid Items within the Container

Listing 6-3 applied some code to the #griditem element that positioned it in the second column, occupying rows 1 to 4. Listing 6-5 repeats this code so you can see what I'm talking about.

Listing 6-5. Positioning of the #griditem Element

```
#griditem {
 grid-column: 2;
 grid-row-start: 1;
 grid-row-end: 4;
}
```

Listing 6-5 shows three attributes I have not yet discussed. `grid-column` defines the column a grid item should occupy. Here, you use a numerical reference to define the column an item should sit in, but as you see later, you could also use a name.

Like `grid-column`, you can also use `grid-row` to define a single row to occupy. In this case, however, you are spanning multiple rows, so instead you use `grid-row-start` and `grid-row-end` to define the beginning and end of the space to occupy with the item.

You may wonder why the code refers to column 4 when it only defines three columns. The answer is in how you think of columns and rows. For the purpose of CSS Grid Layout, each column is defined by the grid line that begins that column; rows work in the same way. If you have three columns, there are actually four column grid lines. Have a look at Figure 6-11 to see this in action.

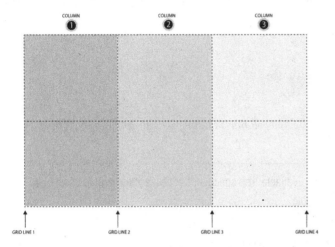

Figure 6-11. *There are four grid lines to define three columns*

`grid-column` and `grid-row` use this same principle, but because each column and row is preceded by an identically numbered grid line, it is not immediately obvious that this is how the numbering system works. It is something to be aware of, especially when you start including gutter columns and rows to separate content areas.

Listing 6-6 shows an example. It defines a total of five columns and three rows, but the intention is only to place content into the principal content areas defined as being bigger than 10px in width or height.

Listing 6-6. CSS Defining Five Columns and Three Rows, Including Gutter Columns and Rows to Separate Content

```
#gridcontainer {
 display: grid;
 grid-template-columns: 150px 10px 150px 10px 150px; /* five columns */
 grid-template-rows: 150px 10px 150px; /* three rows */
}
```

The result of this definition is shown in Figure 6-12; the principal content areas are shaded for clarity. Note that even though there appear to be only three columns and two rows, you have to define the gutters as columns within the grid container. This is important to understand, because if you start positioning grid items using the `grid-column` property, you need to take these extra spacing columns into account. In this example, positioning a grid item in column 2 will result in it occupying the 10px space between the first two principal content columns.

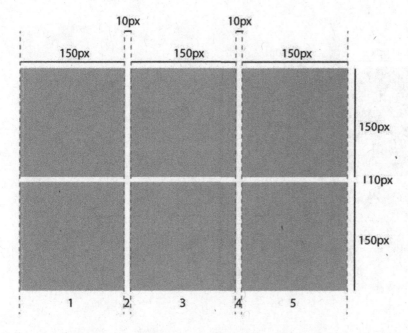

Figure 6-12. *A total of five columns and three rows, with the second and fourth columns set to be 10px wide, and the second row similarly set to occupy 10px of height. This creates the effect of a gutter around the content areas shown shaded*

Shorthand Grid Item Positioning

Typing grid-column-start and grid-column-end can become tiresome quickly; but as ever, CSS has a shorthand syntax available to speed up development. Simply specify the start and end columns (or row for grid-row) using the grid-column property, separating the two values with a forward slash. Listing 6-7 shows this shorthand applied to the example shown in Figure 6-12. The resulting element is positioned as shown in Figure 6-13.

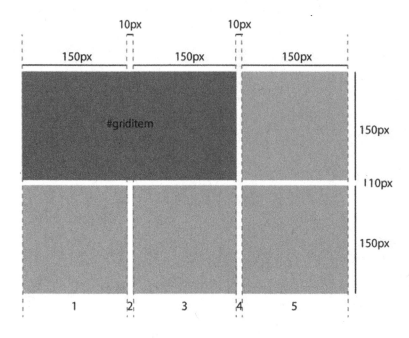

Figure 6-13. *The positioning of element #griditem when the code shown in Listing 6-7 is applied to it*

Listing 6-7. Position and Span of the #griditem Element, Spanning Three Columns and One Row

```
#griditem {
 grid-column: 1 / 4;
 grid-row: 1;
}
```

■ **Caution**   The terms *row* and *column* may make you think of horizontal and vertical layouts, respectively. But in CSS Grid Layout, as with Flexbox, this is only true for horizontal writing modes. In vertical languages such as Japanese, row lays out content from top to bottom.

Positioning Using Grid Area

The grid-area property controls the position of a grid item using the bounding grid lines explicitly, rather than using the column and row metaphor. The syntax is as follows:

grid-area: row-start / column-start / row-end / column-end

This provides an even quicker way to place elements in the grid, by using a coordinate-based approach to positioning. Let's change the code from Listing 6-7 to take advantage of the grid-area property instead of the grid-column and grid-row properties. The resulting code is shown in Listing 6-8.

Listing 6-8. Same Effect as in Listing 6-7, but with Significantly Less Code

```
#griditem {
  grid-area: 1 / 1 / 1 / 4;
}
```

Spanning Multiple Columns or Rows

If you want to treat CSS Grid Layout more like a table-based layout, you can achieve the same effect using the span property. This works by summing the number of columns or rows and assigning the grid item to occupy the correct number of rows and/or columns automatically. Continuing with the example, Listing 6-9 uses span instead of explicitly using grid-area or grid-column-start and grid-column-end. The end is calculated based on the start and span. This is useful when you want to think in terms of spanning multiple columns visually rather than having to maintain the numbers in your head. You do need to keep in mind that any gutter columns still count!

Listing 6-9. Same Result as Listings 6-8 and 6-9, but Using the span Keyword to Define the Grid Item's Size Occupying Three Columns Total

```
#griditem {
  grid-column: 1 / span 3;
  grid-row: 1;
}
```

Naming Grid Lines

If you find yourself frustrated by the need to account for all the superfluous columns and rows introduced by using gutters for padding and margins, CSS Grid Layout offers a practical solution to this problem by allowing you to name individual spans to suit your needs. This is incredibly flexible and useful, and once you are in the habit of using named grid lines, it makes a lot of practical sense for ease of maintenance and legibility of code. The syntax works as follows:

```
grid-template-columns: [name-of-line1] <width> [name-of-line2]
```

The easiest way to explain this is to show it in context, so let's revisit the earlier definition of five columns and three rows from Listing 6-6:

```
#gridcontainer {
  display: grid;
  grid-template-columns: 150px 10px 150px 10px 150px; /* five columns */
  grid-template-rows: 150px 10px 150px /* three rows */
}
```

You can name each grid line by assigning a name in square brackets. Listing 6-10 shows what this looks like in practice. The names can be almost anything that suits you (excepting reserved keywords).

Listing 6-10. CSS from Listing 6-6, with the Sddition of Named Grid Lines

```
#gridcontainer {
 display: grid;
 grid-template-columns: [col1start] 150px [col1end] 10px [col2start] 150px [col2end] 10px
[col3start] 150px [col3end];
 grid-template-rows: [row1start] 150px [row1end] 10px [row2start] 150px [row2end]
}
```

By naming your grid lines, you can now use these names instead of numbers when defining the position of grid items. Listing 6-11 shows the same grid item from Listings 6-7, 6-8, and 6-9, positioned and defined using the names from Listing 6-10.

Listing 6-11. Size and Positioning from Listings 6-7, 6-8, and 6-9, Using the Named Lines Defined in Listing 6-10

```
#griditem {
 grid-column: col1start / col2end;
 grid-row: row1start;
}
```

The result of Listing 6-11 is shown in Figure 6-14. As you can see from the code, this is far more intuitive when you use a sensible naming strategy and assign names that relate to how you might think of columns and rows rather than their position relative to gutter columns and rows.

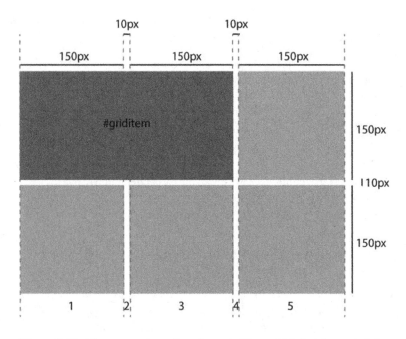

Figure 6-14. *The same net result as shown in Figure 6-13, but the underlying code is potentially easier to understand than earlier listings*

In addition, it is worth pointing out that you can continue to use the span keyword with named grid lines, allowing for further layout flexibility. span continues to observe every column or row defined, however.

Defining Grids with Repeat

The definition of the grid in a grid container can be automated somewhat by using the repeat keyword. The syntax for this is as follows:

```
grid-template-columns: repeat(<number of times to repeat>, <column definitions to repeat>);
```

An example of the repeat keyword in use is shown in Listing 6-12, which defines a grid container with a total of six columns and six rows.

Listing 6-12. Defining Six Columns and Six Rows Using the repeat Keyword

```
#gridcontainer {
  grid-template-column: repeat(3, 150px 10px);
  grid-template-row: repeat(2, 75px 75px 10px);
}
```

The result of the code in Listing 6-12 is shown in Figure 6-15. Again, I have shaded the grid cells to provide clarity.

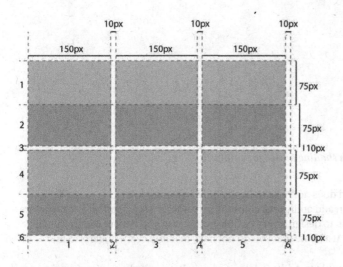

Figure 6-15. *Six columns and six rows defined using the repeat keyword in combination with* grid-template-column *and* grid-template-row

You can also use named grid lines with the repeat keyword, providing further flexibility. An example is shown in Listing 6-13, which defines both a grid container and a grid item.

Listing 6-13. Combining the repeat Keyword with Named Grid Lines to Create a Grid, and Positioning a Grid Item Within It

```
#gridcontainer {
  grid-template-column: repeat(3, [column] 150px [colgutter] 10px);
  grid-template-row: repeat(3, [row] 150px [rowgutter] 10px);
}
```

```
#griditem {
 grid-column: column 2;
 grid-row: row 1;
}
```

The result of Listing 6-13 is shown in Figure 6-16. Cool, huh? You can create a grid system and locate an item within the grid, all in a few short lines of CSS code! And you can still use the span keyword if you want to.

Figure 6-16. *The result of Listing 6-13, with shading added for emphasis*

And there's more! The repeat keyword does not have to be the only argument to the grid-template-column property, so you can add additional columns (or rows for grid-template-row) before or after the repeated section. This allows you to design a very flexible but precise grid system with minimal code. An example is shown in Listing 6-14. Also, note that you do not have to name every single grid line.

Listing 6-14. Building on the Previous Example to Add a Sidebar Column Before the Repeating Section

```
#gridcontainer {
 grid-template-column: [sidebarstart] 200px [sidebarend] 10px repeat(3, [column] 150px
[colgutter] 10px);
 grid-template-row: repeat(3, [row] 150px [rowgutter] 10px);
}
```

The result of Listing 6-14 is shown in Figure 6-17. Something that has not been explicitly shown, but that you should be aware of, is that when repeating definitions result in adjacent named gridlines, the two names are concatenated into a single name. Take the example grid-template-column: repeat(2, [a] 20px [b]). This is equivalent to grid-template-column: [a] 20px [b a] 20px [b];.

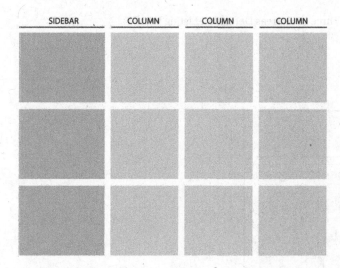

Figure 6-17. *The result of Listing 6-14, incorporating a sidebar defined outside the repeating section of the column specification*

Defining Grid Areas

I have already touched on the difference between a grid cell and a grid area. An area is defined by four grid lines: two column lines and two row lines. These lines do not need to be immediately adjacent, so a grid area can incorporate one or more grid cells. Grid areas are useful for defining the semantic relationship between different parts of a page layout, allowing you to specify which part of the page incorporates the header, sidebar, content area, and footer. Areas are defined using the grid-template-area property, which maps onto an existing set of grid track definitions. Listing 6-15 shows an example of this in action.

Listing 6-15. grid-template-area Defining a Header, Sidebar, and Content Area in the Grid That's Already Defined by the grid-template-columns and grid-template-rows Properties

```
<style>
#gridcontainer {
  display: grid;
grid-template-areas: "header header"
                     "sidebar content"
                     "sidebar content";
grid-template-columns: 150px 1fr;
grid-template-rows: 50px 1fr 50px;
}
</style>
```

Once you have created the grid areas, grid items can be assigned directly to occupy those areas by using the grid-area property; see Listing 6-16. The result of the combined Listings 6-15 and 6-16 is shown in Figure 6-18. Note that the diagram artificially explodes the positioning of the grid cells to make the bounds of each grid area easy to identify.

Listing 6-16. Assigning Three Items to the Three Grid Areas Defined in Listing 6-15

```
#item1 { grid-area: header; }
#item2 { grid-area: sidebar; }
#item3 { grid-area: content; }
```

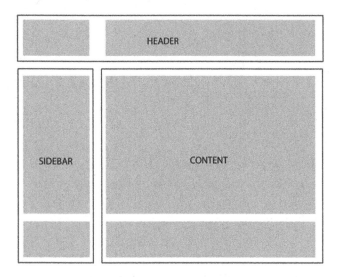

Figure 6-18. *The defined grid areas. Note that I have exploded this diagram, adding extra space between the grid cells to illustrate the bounds of each area*

Controlling the Order of Grid Items

As I have shown, you can position grid items arbitrarily within the grid by using the grid-column and grid-row properties. One of the major benefits of this feature is that it lets you control the visual order of elements on the page independent of their order in code. Just as with Flexbox, this makes it easy to repaginate content to suit different device profiles: responsive design is made simple. It also furthers the campaign to separate style from structure and brings benefits in search engine optimization.

In addition to being able visually to position grid items, you can control the order in which they are rendered to the screen. This functionality uses the same order property available in Flexbox. By using the order property, you can override the default and specify the position of a specific item in the grid render flow. order takes an integer (whole number) value, with lower values rendering before higher values. Negative values are also allowed. order does affect z-index during the painting of elements, so be aware that unless you specifically declare a z-index value for an element, changing its order property will push it forward or back in the stack.

Automatically Flowed Grid Items

Something I have not yet touched on is what happens to grid items if you do not specify a grid-column and grid-row coordinate for every item explicitly. Recall that any child of a grid container is, by default, a grid item. Grid items that are not explicitly positioned and defined are automatically sited and sized, flowing into the grid container in a manner similar to the way flex items flow in a Flexbox container.

By default, the browser adopts the reading direction rules when flowing grid items. In the Latin-based languages, that means rows fill from left to right across the columns until a row is full, and then a new row is started. To help illustrate this, the code in Listing 6-17 contains a grid container and nine child elements.

Listing 6-17. Creating a Grid Container: Child Elements Become Grid Items by Default

```
<style>
 #gridcontainer {
 display: grid;
 grid-template-columns: repeat (3, 150px);
 grid-template-rows: auto;
 }
</style>

<div id="gridcontainer">
 <div class="item">1</div>
 <div class="item">2</div>
 <div class="item">3</div>
 <div class="item">4</div>
 <div class="item">5</div>
 <div class="item">6</div>
 <div class="item">7</div>
 <div class="item">8</div>
 <div class="item">9</div>
</div>
```

By default, the result of Listing 6-17 is as shown in Figure 6-19. Note that using the auto keyword allows the browser to determine how many rows it needs to create in order to accommodate the grid items in the container. You can explicitly ask the browser to flow items into the row context by using the grid-auto-flow property on the grid container element. The default is row, so the code to explicitly set this property is grid-auto-flow: row. The result of changing this property to use a value of column is shown in Figure 6-20.

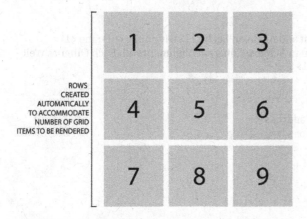

ROWS
CREATED
AUTOMATICALLY
TO ACCOMMODATE
NUMBER OF GRID
ITEMS TO BE RENDERED

Figure 6-19. *The result of Listing 6-17. Grid items are automatically flowed into the row context, although this can also be explicitly set using grid-auto-flow: row*

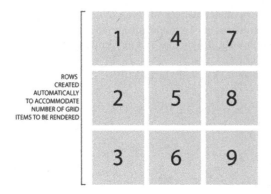

Figure 6-20. *The result of Listing 6-17, but with the grid flow set to a column specifically.* `grid-auto-flow: column` *has been applied to the* `#gridcontainer` *element*

One other nice feature of auto-flow is that it works around any grid items you have explicitly placed on the grid. This means you can push the important elements into their prescribed positions and then allow all the other content on your page or in your app to automatically flow into the surrounding space, completing the layout.

Subgrids

As with Flexbox, separately defined grid containers have no rendering effect on each other. This means if you have two grid containers on the same page, they need not (and will not) refer to each other when rendering and placing content in each respective grid. This is useful in the majority of cases, but sometimes it's helpful to have one grid explicitly refer to and adhere to the grid proportions of the other. For these circumstances, the `subgrid` assignment is available in the CSS Grid Layout specification.

The `subgrid` keyword assigns a grid container element that is a child of an existing grid container to be related to the layout of the parent grid. As such, grid tracks in the subgrid observe and conform to the tracks of the parent grid. This is useful for achieving perfect alignment in forms, as you can see in the example code shown in Listing 6-18.

Listing 6-18. Defining a Grid on the `<ul>` Element and Again on Each `<li>` within the `<ul>`; the `<li>` Elements Are Defined as Subgrids, Allowing Them to Achieve Coherent Alignment with Each Other as Well as with the Overall Parent Grid Defined on the `<ul>`

```
<ul>
 <li><label>Name:</label> <input name="fn">
 <li><label>Address:</label> <input name="address">
 <li><label>Phone:</label> <input name="phone">
</ul>

<style>
ul {
 display: grid;
 grid-auto-flow: row;
 grid-template-columns: auto 1fr;
}
```

```
li {
  display: grid;
  grid: subgrid;
  margin: 0.5em;
  border: solid;
  padding: 0.5em;
}
label {
  grid-column: 1;
}
input {
  grid-column: 2;
}
</style>
```

The result of Listing 6-18 is shown in Figure 6-21. I used the auto-flow option to lay out each list item automatically within the parent grid, along the row-axis flow.

Figure 6-21. *The result of the subgrid in action in Listing 6-18*

In this example, the span of the subgrid <li> items is not explicitly set. The rendering engine automatically notices the use of grid cells in the subgrid and maps this onto the parent grid, adhering to the grid track definitions defined on the parent grid. It is possible to define track spans the same way you have explored with regular grid items.

Explicit vs. Implicit Grids

Until this point, you have dealt exclusively with explicitly defined grids, assigning grid items into predefined grid positions. CSS Grid Layout provides the option to define a grid on the fly, however, by simply assigning a grid item to a position that has not yet been explicitly created.

Under these circumstances, the additional grid tracks are created automatically. For example, if you define a grid container as grid-template-columns: 100px 100px 100px 100px and then apply a grid item to occupy grid-column: 5, the extra column necessary to position the grid item is created to accommodate the grid item. Listing 6-17 uses the keyword auto specifically to request that the browser apply this behavior to grid rows, but, strictly speaking, that is not necessary. Personally, I think it is nice to be specific and even verbose if it helps avoid doubt, so I tend not to rely on default values or behavior where practical. You can make up your own mind about what suits you!

Aligning Items to the Grid

Grid items can be aligned relative to the grid using the align-items property applied to the grid container. Possible values for align-items are as follows:

- stretch: The default. Expands the item to fill the space defined by the cell.

- start: Aligns the content to the start of the grid cell relative to the flow context. The item is sized to accommodate the content.

- end: Just like start, but aligns to the end of the cell rather than the beginning.

- center: Aligns the content to the center of the grid cell, expanding to fill as much of the cell as necessary to accommodate the content of the grid item.

In addition to align-items, which works along the flow context, CSS Grid Layout allows for justify-items, which works across the flow context. The same set of values is acceptable for both properties, and they work in the exact same manner, either with or perpendicular to the flow.

Figure 6-22 shows the result of the four alignment options for align-items. Note that in this example, the flow context is along the column axis, and each grid item occupies five rows. I have sized the individual items as if they were filled with enough content to effectively take up about half the space afforded by those five rows.

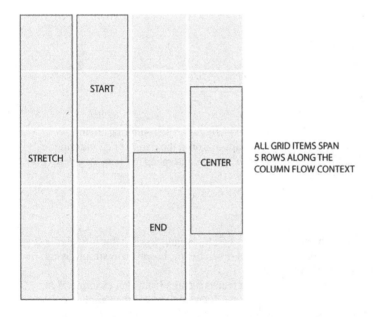

Figure 6-22. The four alignment options

Finally, there is also the option to set alignment on a per-item basis using the justify-self and align-self properties. These properties support the same four values but are assigned to the grid item rather than the grid container.

How to Use CSS Grid Layout

By now, you should have a clear idea of just how powerful and useful CSS Grid Layout is. It can single-handedly solve many common layout issues, and in many respects it's the one CSS module designers have been crying out for since the first days of the Web. As a result, it is ever so tempting to think of CSS Grid Layout as offering the ultimate solution to every layout need.

It is true that CSS Grid Layout *will* offer a nirvana of sorts for the seasoned web designer. Note my emphasis on the word *will*! Once the issues I'm about to discuss are dealt with, CSS Grid Layout will be a wonderful and incredibly useful addition to your toolset. Common usage scenarios will include the following:

- Magazine-style layouts

- Pinterest-type web apps

- Areas of a page where you want to reorder content from the markup order (although note that Flexbox also allows you to do this)

- Apps, especially when using a web view and targeting a range of device profiles

- Forms and form elements layout

Of course, that is just the beginning of what a grid layout is good for. Much of the design currently on the Web could be rendered using CSS Grid Layout, if only it were possible to use it reliably across different browsers.

Browser Support

As I mentioned at the beginning of this chapter, browser support for CSS Grid Layout is very poor currently. Microsoft has helped define the specification and is to date the only vendor to have a partially working implementation ready and available to test in a consumer-facing browser release, but this will change rapidly once the specification becomes fully stable. Note that you can access some of the current specification in the Canary version of Chrome at the time of writing.

As ever, for the current situation, you should refer to and periodically check http://caniuse.com/#search=grid. This site is maintained to provide a snapshot of the latest browser support for CSS Grid Layout.

Fallback Options and Polyfills

As with all non-supported CSS, browsers that don't understand the CSS Grid Layout properties fall back to their default values for each element. This means, typically, that structural items such as <div>, <section>, and <article> display as block-level elements, whereas inline elements such as <span> revert to their default inline-level behavior. You can use this to your advantage to handle older browsers or if you prefer to polyfill using one of the numerous grid systems that rely on JavaScript to position and size elements. Be aware that because there are some crossover properties in common with Flexbox, the fallback options may be less predictable than you expect. The Modernizr JavaScript library allows you to test for browser support; you can find out more at http://modernizr.com.

Summary

CSS Grid Layout offers potentially the most exciting layout options of all the new-to-CSS3 modules. However, it is not yet ready to be used in the wild—unless you are willing to write a lot of JavaScript fallbacks and/or polyfills.

Nevertheless, we are on the cusp of the grid revolution. Once the main browsers offer support, designers will have an extremely flexible layout tool at their disposal that is engineered to work responsively. CSS Grid Layout will deal with many of the layout headaches that have troubled designers for the past 20 years, ridding us of the laborious and elaborate workarounds that have been necessary in the past. Unfortunately, browser support just is not there, so it is not safe to use CSS Grid Layout on the Web—yet.

CHAPTER 7

CSS Regions Layout

CSS Regions Layout makes it easy to flow content from one box to another without having to worry about how the content will fit inside each container.

■ **Note** This module is still in Editor's Draft status and is subject to change. Be sure to check the latest W3C documentation at `www.w3.org/TR/css3-regions/` for details about the current syntax and specification. Also check the code for this book in the Source Code tab on the book's page at `Apress.com/9781430265023`.

What Is CSS Regions Layout?

CSS Regions Layout provides an advanced solution for controlling content flow across different containers. The individual containers don't have to be next to each other in the layout, so it's easy to create magazine-style layouts that remain flexible for content changes.

CSS Regions Layout doesn't control layout of elements on the page, only the way content flows between elements. This allows the module to be used with any layout model in the CSS specification.

That said, with the addition of a useful pseudo-element selector, you can use a number of properties to style content flowing into a region. I discuss the `::region()` selector and the `selector` method it replaces later in this chapter.

The biggest challenge you face if you want to use CSS Regions Layout today is the patchy browser support. Both Safari and Chrome offer support, but Chrome doesn't enable CSS Regions Layout by default. Internet Explorer 10 also supports CSS Regions Layout, but the source content can only come from an `iframe`. Of course, just as with many of the new CSS3 layout modules, you can use polyfill solutions to bring support to all browsers; I talk about these options later in this chapter.

An Example

The easiest way to get an understanding of what CSS Regions Layout can do is to jump straight into an example. Figure 7-1 shows a simple layout that has three boxes. The content of each of these boxes is controlled using CSS Regions Layout, but the layout is set using a combination of CSS2.1 absolute positioning and CSS3 transformations.

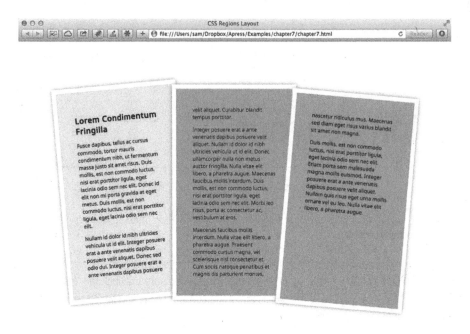

Figure 7-1. *The layout is controlled by CSS2.1 and CSS3 transformations. The content is controlled by CSS Regions Layout.*

Listing 7-1 shows the HTML markup used to create this example. Notice that there are two distinct areas in the markup:

- The text content of the page in an `<article>` element
- Three `<div>` elements that contain no renderable content

Listing 7-1. HTML Markup for the Example Shown in Figure 7-1

```
<body>
 <article>
  <h1>Lorem Condimentum Fringilla</h1>
  <p>Fusce dapibus, tellus ac cursus commodo, tortor mauris condimentum nibh, ut fermentum
  massa justo sit amet risus. Duis mollis, est non commodo luctus, nisi erat porttitor
  ligula, eget lacinia odio sem nec elit. Donec id elit non mi porta gravida at eget metus.
  Duis mollis, est non commodo luctus, nisi erat porttitor ligula, eget lacinia odio sem nec
  elit.</p>
   <p>Nullam id dolor id nibh ultricies vehicula ut id elit. Integer posuere erat a ante
   venenatis dapibus posuere velit aliquet. Donec sed odio dui. Integer posuere erat a ante
   venenatis dapibus posuere velit aliquet. Curabitur blandit tempus porttitor.</p>
```

```
<p>Integer posuere erat a ante venenatis dapibus posuere velit aliquet. Nullam id
dolor id nibh ultricies vehicula ut id elit. Donec ullamcorper nulla non metus auctor
fringilla. Nulla vitae elit libero, a pharetra augue. Maecenas faucibus mollis interdum.
Duis mollis, est non commodo luctus, nisi erat porttitor ligula, eget lacinia odio sem
nec elit. Morbi leo risus, porta ac consectetur ac, vestibulum at eros.</p>
<p>Maecenas faucibus mollis interdum. Nulla vitae elit libero, a pharetra augue. Praesent
commodo cursus magna, vel scelerisque nisl consectetur et. Cum sociis natoque penatibus
et magnis dis parturient montes, nascetur ridiculus mus. Maecenas sed diam eget risus
varius blandit sit amet non magna.</p>
<p>Duis mollis, est non commodo luctus, nisi erat porttitor ligula, eget lacinia odio sem
nec elit. Etiam porta sem malesuada magna mollis euismod. Integer posuere erat a ante
venenatis dapibus posuere velit aliquet. Nullam quis risus eget urna mollis ornare vel eu
leo. Nulla vitae elit libero, a pharetra augue.</p>
</article>
<div id="box1"><!-- no content --></div>
<div id="box2"><!-- no content --></div>
<div id="box3"><!-- no content --></div>
</body>
```

When you use CSS Regions Layout, the content flows from an element (or range of elements) into one or more regions. The element that provides the content isn't rendered in the browser, so the <article> in Listing 7-1 doesn't appear directly in the render shown in Figure 7-1.

Let's look at the CSS code used to create this layout. Listing 7-2 shows the complete stylesheet to render this page. You can download the source code for this example, and all the other examples in this book, at http://www.apress.com.

Listing 7-2. CSS Code Used in Conjunction with Listing 7-1

```
body {
 font-family: 'Noto Sans', sans-serif;
 font-size: 62.5%;
}
article {
 -webkit-flow-into: article;
 -ms-flow-into: article;
 flow-into: article;
 font-size: 1.2em;
}
#box1, #box2, #box3 {
 -webkit-flow-from: article;
 -ms-flow-from: article;
 flow-from: article;
}
#box1, #box2, #box3 {
 padding: 4em;
 border: 10px solid #fff;
 position: absolute;
 width: 200px;
 height: 400px;
 background: #fff;
 box-shadow: 0px 0px 10px #999;
}
```

```
#box1 {
 background: #f9e719;
 top: 100px;
 left: 100px;
 -webkit-transform: rotate(-5deg);
 transform: rotate(-5deg);
}
#box2 {
 background: #92f919;
 top: 100px;
 left: 370px;
}
#box3 {
 background: #19d2f9;
 top: 120px;
 left: 640px;
 -webkit-transform: rotate(5deg);
 transform: rotate(5deg);
}
```

This example uses the flow-into and flow-from properties to create regions. The three <div>s with IDs of box1, box2, and box3 each become a region, and the <article> element effectively becomes a content store and isn't rendered directly on the page.

The benefit of using CSS Regions Layout here is that if you want to update the content later, you can simply edit the HTML in the <article> element. The content will reflow across the three defined regions without the need for any manual formatting.

■ **Note**   The first example shows the different vendor-prefixed versions of the flow-into and flow-from properties. The remaining examples omit these vendor-specific prefixed versions of the properties to avoid clutter. Until the specification is complete, you need to include prefixed versions of the properties in your own code.

Browser Support

CSS Regions Layout is quite a new specification, originally proposed and promoted by Adobe in 2011. Despite this, there have already been several iterations to the proposal, and some browsers offer reasonably mature support. Safari version 6.1 and above works with vendor prefixes, as does Chrome (once support is enabled by entering about:flags into the address bar and enabling Experimental Web Platform Features). Internet Explorer 10 and above also support CSS Regions Layout, although the source markup must be contained in an iframe. At the time of publication, Firefox doesn't have any support for CSS Regions Layout, and some engineers who work on Firefox have gone on record saying they have no plans to implement the proposal. This is because the team of developers behind Firefox believe there are problems with the CSS Regions Layout specification, specifically as the proposed CSS Overflow module deals with some similar layout issues. So, at this point there is reason to believe this may be an issue for future development.

■ **Tip**   Check http://caniuse.com/#feat=css-regions to view a table showing the latest level of browser support.

Syntax and Structure

The syntax for CSS Regions Layout is very simple. There are only two primary properties:

- `flow-into`
- `flow-from`

Each of these properties takes a named argument that defines, in the case of `flow-into`, or calls on, in the case of `flow-from`, a flow context. A flow context can be given any name, as long as it starts with a letter and contains valid CSS characters.

flow-into

Once a flow context is defined, all elements assigned with a `flow-into` property matching that assignment contribute their contents to the flow. They are also removed from the visual layout of the page.

The order in which content is assigned into the flow is determined by the order of the HTML markup, chronologically. This is shown in Listing 7-3, where three different content areas are assigned to the same flow context in a different order than their position in the markup.

Listing 7-3. Order of Content in the Flow Is Determined by the Markup Alone

```
<article id="article1"> <h1>Article 1</h1>
 <p>...</p>
</article>
<article id="article2"><h1>Article 2</h1>
 <p>...</p>
</article>
<article id="article3"><h1>Article 3</h1>
 <p>...</p>
</article>
<div id="layout"><!-- single content container --></div>
<style>
 #article1, #article3 {
 flow-into: reorderedcontent;
}
#article2 {
 flow-into: reorderedcontent;
}
#layout {
 flow-from: reorderedcontent;
}
</style>
```

The result of Listing 7-3 is shown in Figure 7-2. Note that the articles have not been reordered in the output, even though they are defined in the order #article1, #article3, #article2 when assigning the flow-into property.

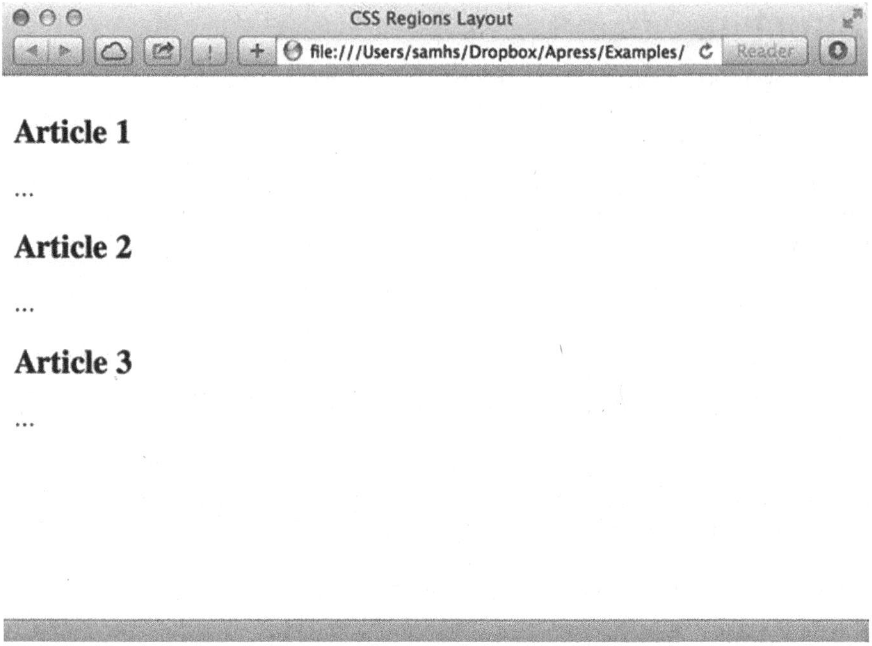

Figure 7-2. *The order of content is defined by the HTML markup, not the CSS assignment to a named flow.*

It's important to take care when assigning elements into a flow to avoid unintended consequences. Take the example of a table, which could be assigned to a flow using the code shown in Listing 7-4.

Listing 7-4. Moving a Table and Its Contents into a Flow Named `table-content`

```
table {flow-into: table-content}
```

As you might expect, this rule takes all tables in the document and moves them into a flow named `table-content`. The tables themselves, in addition to all contents are moved into the flow, retain their separation from other elements. The code shown in Listing 7-5 only selects direct child elements in tables to be moved into the flow.

Listing 7-5. Moving All Direct Children of the Table Element(s) into the Flow

```
table > * {flow-into: table-content}
```

This allows all table rows in the document, sourced from across multiple source tables, to be rendered together in a single table. That's a really useful capability. Note, however, that it leaves behind the <table> as an empty element that is still rendered in the document; so if you have styles applied, they still appear.

Consider Listing 7-6, though, and you'll see that this power can be accidentally used with unintended consequences.

Listing 7-6. Moving All Descendants of the Table Element(s) into the Flow at the Same Level

```
table * {flow-into: table-content}
```

The net effect of the code in Listing 7-6 would be to render the contents of all tables in a flat list, rather than a nested tree as a table would usually render. This is almost certainly not what you would expect.

The lesson to take away is that specificity is especially important when dealing with CSS Regions Layout. Be as specific as you can be to avoid unexpected results.

■ **Note** Another potentially unexpected consequence of CSS Regions Layout is that any white space surrounding an element is not moved into the flow, causing inline elements added to the flow to render adjacent to each other.

---

flow-from

The `flow-from` property allows arbitrarily positioned containers to form a chain of regions through which a flow of content is rendered. Figure 7-3 shows how this can be used to create magazine-style layouts without the need to render content into individual containers.

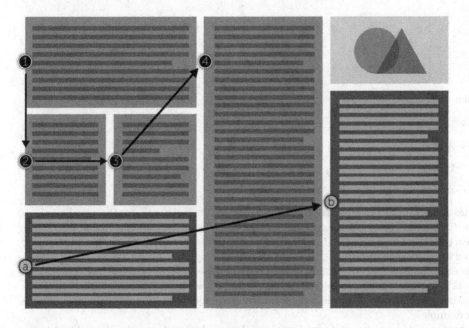

***Figure 7-3.** Two named flows forming a magazine-style layout*

The `flow-from` property has only two limitations:

- The named flow must exist, having been defined using the `flow-into` property on one or more elements in the document.

- The container the `flow-from` property is applied to cannot already be a region.

A page can contain an unlimited number of named flows and an unlimited number of regions. If a named flow is defined but empty, the element does not render visually. It's worth noting that cyclical assignments of named flows can't be used either; an element cannot contain a `flow-into` and `flow-from` property with the same named flow.

Controlling Break Points

When content is moved from the document flow into a CSS Regions Layout flow context, the point at which content breaks between different container regions is determined by the size of those regions. This can produce potentially undesirable breaks as the content flows across multiple regions. To help deal with this problem, the specification defines three additional properties that are supported in conjunction with flow-from:

- break-before
- break-after
- break-inside

Each of these properties can be applied to any HTML element that is rendered in a CSS region, controlling breaks in rendering across different regions. There are a number of different potential values:

- auto
- always
- avoid
- left
- right
- page
- column
- region
- avoid-page
- avoid-column
- avoid-region

The properties and possible values for break-before, break-after, and break-inside have been extended from the CSS3 Multi-columns Layout module, which is discussed in Chapter 4. Rather than exhaustively repeat the explanation provided in Chapter 4, I summarize here and highlight the additional options introduced with CSS Regions Layout.

Each of the break options, with the exception of auto, defines a specific point at which the content can or cannot break before continuing to render in the next region in the chain. The left, right, page, and avoid-page values only apply to printed pages, forcing contents to render when printed so that content falls on a left page, for example.

The column, region, avoid-column, and avoid-region values each allow for an element to break before, after, or inside a column or region, or to avoid doing so. The region option is peculiar to CSS Regions Layout. Figure 7-4 shows the effect of the break-before:region option when applied to a heading tag.

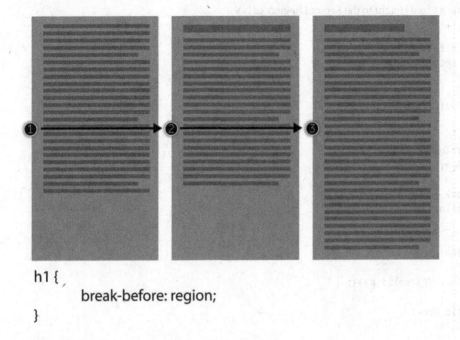

```
h1 {
        break-before: region;
}
```

Figure 7-4. <h1>s are forced to break before a region

Choosing when and how to break content between regions on the page can provide fine control over a page's appearance while retaining the benefits of abstracted content. By default, all CSS layout containers expand to fit their contents, just as with normal inline HTML contents. This is useful when you're dealing with an unknown amount of content but less practical when you're aiming for a pixel-based layout. Figure 7-5 shows the effect of applying a `height` attribute to a region in combination with the `break-after` property. The source code for this example is shown in Listing 7-7.

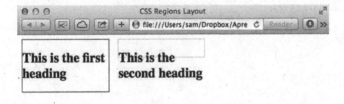

Figure 7-5. *The second region does not expand to fit its contents*

Listing 7-7. Applying a Fixed Height to the Second Region <div>

```
<article>
 <h2>This is the first heading</h2>
 <h2>This is the second heading</h2>
</article>
<div id="region1"><!-- empty --></div>
<div id="region2"><!-- empty --></div>
<style>
 article h2 {
  flow-into: overfloweg;
  break-after: always;
 }
 #region1, #region2 {
  flow-from: overfloweg;
  float: left;
  width: 10em;
  margin-right: 1em;
 }
 #region1 {  border: 1px solid #333; }
 #region2 {
  border: 1px solid #ccc;
  height: 2em;
 }
</style>
```

■ **Note**   This example doesn't render properly in WebKit browsers due to a problem with `break-after: always`.

region-fragment and Overflow

The `region-fragment` property provides control over how the final region of a named flow behaves. Suppose you have a flow running across the regions shown in Figure 7-6.

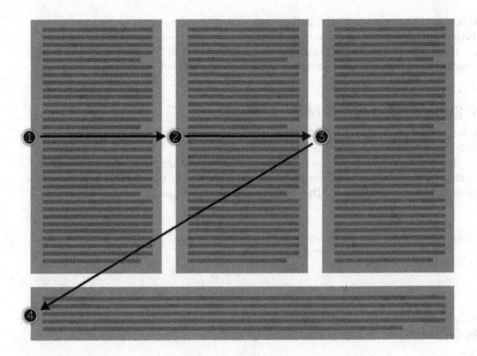

Figure 7-6. *A simple CSS Regions Layout flow example*

The `region-fragment` property defines how content should be rendered if it occupies more space than will fit in the final region, marked as region 4 in Figure 7-6. There are two possible values for `region-fragment`:

- `auto`
- `break`

`auto` allows the overflowing content to render as part of the final region. `break` removes the overflowing content from the final region as if there were another region to flow into.

This is not the same as `overflow: hidden`, which retains the content in the region but hides the overflowing content. Figure 7-7 shows the differences between the two possible values, combined with `overflow: hidden`. Note that `region-fragment` does not affect the size of the final region, so it does not have any affect on a region that resizes to accommodate content (that is, with no set `height` property in this example).

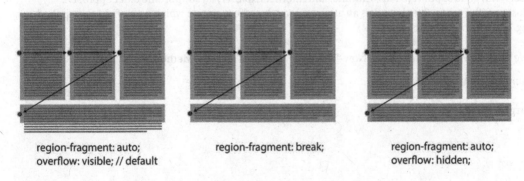

region-fragment: auto;   region-fragment: break;   region-fragment: auto;
overflow: visible; // default   overflow: hidden;

Figure 7-7. *Examples of how different `region-fragment` options render in the browser*

Because CSS Regions Layout doesn't deal with the position or layout of the elements being used to render content, it's important to understand that regions render region fragments according to the layout properties applied. If you use CSS Flexible Box Layout in conjunction with CSS Regions Layout, for example, you may have content overflowing on the horizontal axis rather than the vertical.

The New Region Styling Approach

If you remember the introduction to this chapter, I said that CSS Regions Layout doesn't deal with the way content looks—only how it flows. This is true, but it's not the whole truth.

The new ::region() pseudo-selector allows visual characteristics to be set on content in a flow that renders in a particular region. These visual properties are largely inline and do not affect the document flow, but some can impact on block-level rendering. The syntax for using the ::region() selector is shown in Listing 7-8.

Listing 7-8. Syntax to Assign Rules to Content Rendering in a Specific Region Element

```
<region-element>::region(selector) {
 // styles
}
```

An example of a real-world usage scenario is shown in Listing 7-9, which selects all paragraphs rendered from the flow in #region1 and applies a margin-right of 2em.

Listing 7-9. Applies a Right Margin of 2em to All <p> Elements Rendered from the Flow in #region1

```
#region1::region(p) {
 margin-right: 2em;
}
```

Unfortunately, there's currently very little browser support for this part of the CSS Regions Layout specification.

The Old Region Styling Approach

When the original specification for CSS Regions Layout was drawn up in 2011, it called for a selector method to allow for styling content in a region similar to the way @media queries work. Although this has been replaced by ::region(), many of the examples on the Web continue to use this syntax, and the three browsers with good support (Safari, Chrome, and Internet Explorer) all support the older approach.

Just as with @media, @region takes an argument to select the region to which a set of styles is applied. Listing 7-10 shows the basic syntax.

Listing 7-10. Example Syntax for the Now-Deprecated @region Selector Method

```
@region #region1 {
 p {
   margin-right: 2em;
 }
}
```

This example re-creates the example from Listing 7-9 using the old syntax. The CSS selects the region with an ID of region1 and applies a margin-right of 2em to any paragraphs rendered in it.

I recommend that you avoid using this syntax for production web sites; but at the time of publication, browser support for ::region() is nonexistent. In contrast, support for @region is good in both Safari and Chrome. You need to decide for yourself whether you want to use the old or the new syntax or avoid using it altogether.

Available Selectors

Not every CSS property can be applied to elements selected with ::region() or @region. The properties that can be assigned are as follows:

- font properties
- color
- opacity
- background
- word-spacing
- letter-spacing
- text-decoration
- text-transform
- line-height
- alignment and justification properties
- border
- border-radius
- border-image
- margin
- padding
- text-shadow
- box-shadow
- box-decoration-break
- width

Visual Characteristics of CSS Regions Layout

No limitations are imposed by CSS Regions Layout regarding how you style or position regions on the page. The module works well in conjunction with all CSS2.1 and CSS3 layout approaches, so you can combine CSS Regions Layout with CSS Multi-columns Layout, CSS Grids Layout, CSS Flexible Box Layout, and floating and absolutely positioned elements.

Polyfill Options

As you've seen, browser support for CSS Regions Layout isn't anything like universal, and it's unlikely that this will change in the near future. As a web designer, this is one of the most frustrating aspects of seeing new CSS modules being developed; we're all desperate to try the new features, but they're not ready for prime time.

As the primary proponents of CSS Regions Layout, Adobe has developed a polyfill that provides support for much of the specification in browsers that haven't adopted the proposals yet. You can download the polyfill source code from `http://adobe-webplatform.github.io/css-regions-polyfill/`. And other than using `-adobe-` as a prefix to your CSS Regions Layout code, you can use the code examples shown in this chapter exactly as printed.

Real-World Example

As discussed, CSS Regions Layout doesn't have an impact on the layout of elements in a page design. It can be used with any of the other CSS layout modules discussed in this book. So, rather than provide an example of one of those modules, I've incorporated another new module proposed by Adobe for this brief example: CSS Shapes.

The CSS Shapes module is discussed further in Chapter 10, so I don't go into detail here, but it makes for a fun, if slightly whimsical, example of how CSS Regions Layout can help solve particular layout problems. Figure 7-8 shows a mockup created in Adobe Illustrator: a simple magazine-style layout where two text areas wrap perfectly around an image of a guitar. This example uses CSS Regions Layout to render the content so that it automatically flows across the two text boxes and CSS Shapes to create the boxes that contain the text.

The development of
THE GIBSON LES PAUL

The Gibson Les Paul was the result of a design collaboration between Gibson Guitar Corporation and the late jazz guitarist and electronics inventor Les Paul. In 1950, with the introduction of the radically innovative Fender Telecaster to the musical market, solid-body electric guitars became a public craze (hollow-body electric guitars have more acoustic resonance but are, therefore, more prone to amplifier feedback and have less natural note duration "sustain".) In reaction, Gibson Guitar president Ted McCarty brought guitarist Les Paul into the company as a consultant. Les Paul was a respected innovator who had been experimenting with guitar design for years to benefit his own music. In fact, he had hand-built a solid-body prototype called "The Log", a design widely considered the first solid-body Spanish guitar ever built, as opposed to the "Hawaiian", or lap-steel guitar. This guitar is known as "The Log" because the solid core is a pine block whose width and depth are a little more than the width of the fretboard; conventional hollow guitar sides were added for shape (Image 2), a design similar to the popular Gibson ES-335 semi-hollowbody guitar introduced in 1958. Although numerous other prototypes and limited-production solid-body models by other makers have since surfaced, it is known that in 1945–1946, Les Paul had approached Gibson with "The Log" prototype, but his solid body design was rejected.[8][9]

In 1951, this initial rejection became a design collaboration between the Gibson Guitar Corporation and Les Paul. It was agreed that the new Les Paul guitar was to be an expensive, well-made instrument in Gibson's tradition.[10] Although recollections differ regarding who contributed what to the Les Paul design, it was far from a market replica of Fender models. Founded in 1902, Gibson began offering electric hollow-body guitars in the 1930s, such as the ES-150; at minimum, these hollow-body electric models provided a set of basic design cues for the new Gibson solid-body, including a more traditionally curved body shape than offered by competitor Fender, and a glued-in ("set-in") neck, in contrast to Fender's bolt-on neck.

The significance of Les Paul's contributions to his Gibson guitar design remains controversial. The book "50 Years of the Gibson Les Paul" limits Paul's contributions to two: advice on the trapeze tailpiece, and a preference for color (stating that Paul preferred gold as "it looks expensive", and a second choice of black because "it makes your fingers appear to move faster on the box", and "looks classy—like a tuxedo").[11]

Additionally, Gibson's president Ted McCarty states that the Gibson Guitar Corporation merely approached Les Paul for the right to imprint the musician's name on the headstock to increase model sales, and that in 1951, Gibson showed Paul a nearly finished instrument. McCarty also claims that design discussions with Les Paul were limited to the tailpiece and the fitting of a maple cap over the mahogany body for increased density and sustain, which Les Paul had requested reversed.

Text and image from http://en.wikipedia.org/wiki/Gibson_Les_Paul

Figure 7-8. *A mockup of a magazine-style layout, created in Adobe Illustrator*

The HTML Markup

The HTML markup needed for this page is extremely simple. You have a container for the page, which itself has two text boxes. Listing 7-11 shows the HTML code for the page and includes text content taken from Wikipedia's article on the subject matter.

Listing 7-11. HTML Code for the Magazine-Style Layout Page (Content from Wikipedia)

```
<div id="container">
 <div id="title"><h1><span>the development of</span> <br />The Gibson Les Paul</h1></div>
 <div id="box1"><!-- left side of the guitar --></div>
 <div id="box2"><!-- right side of the guitar --></div>
</div>
<article id="content">
```

```
<p> The Gibson Les Paul was the result of a design collaboration between Gibson Guitar
Corporation and the late jazz guitarist and electronics inventor Les Paul. In 1950, with
the introduction of the radically innovative Fender Telecaster to the musical market,
solid-body electric guitars became a public craze (hollow-body electric guitars have more
acoustic resonance but are, therefore, more prone to amplifier feedback and have less
natural note duration "sustain".) In reaction, Gibson Guitar president Ted McCarty brought
guitarist Les Paul into the company as a consultant. Les Paul was a respected innovator
who had been experimenting with guitar design for years to benefit his own music. In fact,
he had hand-built a solid-body prototype called "The Log", a design widely considered the
first solid-body Spanish guitar ever built, as opposed to the "Hawaiian", or lap-steel
guitar. This guitar is known as "The Log" because the solid core is a pine block whose
width and depth are a little more than the width of the fretboard; conventional hollow
guitar sides were added for shape (Image 2), a design similar to the popular Gibson
ES-335 semi-hollowbody guitar introduced in 1958. Although numerous other prototypes and
limited-production solid-body models by other makers have since surfaced, it is known that
in 1945-1946, Les Paul had approached Gibson with "The Log" prototype, but his solid body
design was rejected.[8][9]</p>
<p>In 1951, this initial rejection became a design collaboration between the Gibson
Guitar Corporation and Les Paul. It was agreed that the new Les Paul guitar was to be an
expensive, well-made instrument in Gibson's tradition.[10] Although recollections differ
regarding who contributed what to the Les Paul design, it was far from a market replica of
Fender models. Founded in 1902, Gibson began offering electric hollow-body guitars in the
1930s, such as the ES-150; at minimum, these hollow-body electric models provided a set of
basic design cues for the new Gibson solid-body, including a more traditionally curved body
shape than offered by competitor Fender, and a glued-in ("set-in") neck, in contrast to
Fender's bolt-on neck.</p>
<p>The significance of Les Paul's contributions to his Gibson guitar design remains
controversial. The book "50 Years of the Gibson Les Paul" limits Paul's contributions
to two: advice on the trapeze tailpiece, and a preference for color (stating that Paul
preferred gold as "it looks expensive", and a second choice of black because "it makes your
fingers appear to move faster on the box", and "looks classy—like a tuxedo").[11]</p>
<p>Additionally, Gibson's president Ted McCarty states that the Gibson Guitar Corporation
merely approached Les Paul for the right to imprint the musician's name on the headstock to
increase model sales, and that in 1951, Gibson showed Paul a nearly finished instrument.
McCarty also claims that design discussions with Les Paul were limited to the tailpiece and
the fitting of a maple cap over the mahogany body for increased density and sustain, which
Les Paul had requested reversed.</p>
</article>
```

The CSS Shapes and CSS Regions Layout Code

As mentioned, I'm not going to explain the CSS Shapes code in this example; you can read more about the proposal later in the book. Listing 7-12 shows the CSS code that creates both the shapes and the regions. Like the text, the guitar image is from Wikipedia.

Listing 7-12. CSS Used to Render Both CSS Regions Layout and CSS Shapes

```
#container {
 position: relative;
 margin: auto;
 width: 960px;
```

```
   height: 1200px;
   background: transparent url(guitar.jpg) no-repeat bottom left;
}
#container h1 {
 position: absolute;
 top: 300px;
 left: 50px;
 font-weight: 100;
 font-size: 2.2em;
 text-transform: uppercase;
 margin: 0;
 padding: 0;
}
#container h1 span {
 font-size: 0.5em;
 text-transform: none;
}
article {
 -webkit-flow-into: article;
 flow-into: article;
}
#box1, #box2 {
 -webkit-flow-from: article;
 flow-from: article;
}

#box1 {
 position: absolute;
 top: 385px;
 left: 50px;
 width: 390px;
 height: 600px;
 overflow: hidden;
 -webkit-shape-inside: polygon(0% 0%, 100% 0%, 100% 36%, 70% 50%, 80% 70%, 50% 100%, 0%
100%, 0% 0%);
}

#box2 {
 position: absolute;
 top: 400px;
 right: 50px;
 width: 420px;
 height: 600px;
 overflow: hidden;
 -webkit-shape-inside: polygon(3% 0%, 5% 50%, 28% 50%, 20% 68%, 35% 85%, 45% 100%, 100%
100%, 100% 0%, 0% 0%);
}
```

■ **Note** This example only renders correctly in Chrome (with experimental features enabled) or the nightly build of WebKit.

The Result

Figure 7-9 shows the result of the HTML in Listing 7-11 and the CSS in Listing 7-12, as rendered in Chrome with experimental features enabled. This isn't a perfect re-creation of my original mockup, but with some additional region-specific content styling, it would be a very close match.

Figure 7-9. *The result of the code in Listings 7-11 and 7-12, rendered in Chrome*

Summary

CSS Regions Layout offers a leap forward in the way designers can position content boxes on a page, abstracting the content of an element from its presentation. This opens up a range of potentially exciting new layout possibilities.

Unfortunately, universal browser support is still a long way off, especially given that Firefox appears unlikely to implement the proposal in the near future. Polyfill options can provide the functionality in browsers that don't have native support, but as with any workaround, these rely on scripting (which can be disabled by the user). At some point in the future, CSS Regions Layout may play a large part in the toolkit of the web designer, but currently it's more an exciting glimpse of what's to come.

CHAPTER 8

■ ■ ■

Supporting Older Browsers

One of the basic tenets of the Web is that there are many different device profiles, including bleeding-edge, bang-up-to-date smartphones, tablets, and laptops, and older corporate desktop systems. This is great for the democracy of the Internet as a whole, but it creates headaches for web designers, especially when we're all keen to adopt the latest standards and make full use of them in our pages.

When you're crafting a new layout for a web site and want to adopt one of the CSS3 layout modules, where does this problem leave you? How can you use the new modules while avoiding making your page render in an unreadable manner for users of older browsers?

Fortunately, in most cases it's possible to adopt a progressive enhancement approach (see Figure 8-1) to supporting these older, out-of-date browsers; by applying a core basic layout that works without any of the new layout modules, you can then layer the good stuff on top. Browsers that understand the new modules will adhere to the enhanced rules, and those that don't will simply ignore them, sticking with the core fallback layout.

■ **Tip** It's well worth regularly checking your visitor statistics and making an informed decision about how much effort to put into supporting older browsers. If you only get five visits per year from someone still running Internet Explorer 8, it may be time to stop expending energy on making your site work for that browser!

Figure 8-1. *A useful article on the A List Apart web site, found at http://alistapart.com/article/ understandingprogressiveenhancement, that explains the concept of progressive enhancement in detail*

© Sam Hampton-Smith 2016

S. Hampton-Smith, *Pro CSS3 Layout Techniques*, DOI 10.1007/978-1-4302-6503-0_8

When There's No Alternative

Although progressive enhancement works in many cases, it isn't always a satisfactory solution to the problem of supporting older browsers. Sometimes the project dictates that you must adopt a layout that isn't possible without some level of support for a particular CSS module or paradigm.

Under these circumstances, there's an alternative approach that works hand in hand with progressive enhancement to either programmatically build support for modules into an older browser or work around the lack of support using scripts or hacks. This method of dealing with the inadequacies of older software is called *polyfilling*.

Wikipedia describes a *polyfill* as "downloadable code which provides facilities that are not built into a web browser. It implements technology that a developer expects the browser to provide natively, providing a more uniform API landscape. For example, many features of HTML5 are not supported by versions of Internet Explorer older than version 8 or 9, but can be used by web pages if those pages install a polyfill." Related terms that are used to describe a similar approach to dealing with nonsupporting browsers include *shiv* and *shim*. The basic premise is the same, however, regardless of what you name the approach. JavaScript is typically used to interrogate the browser for support for a particular feature, and if support isn't present, it either provides CSS hooks to allow for alternative styling (in the case of progressive enhancement) or provides workaround support in the form of pseudo-native adherence to the standard.

Modernizr

As you'll see during the course of this chapter, many different polyfill solutions and approaches to polyfilling are available, but all of them rely on using some method of detecting browser support for a specific feature and, assuming lack of support is found, providing an alternative. The basis for this approach is feature detection, and perhaps the best-known tool for this purpose is the Modernizr library (see Figure 8-2).

Figure 8-2. The Modernizr web page: `http://modernizr.com`

Modernizr is a JavaScript library that allows you to use feature-detection to determine whether the browser being used to access your web site can render specific types of content or support particular features. The library works by checking for support in the browser against a series of tests. For example, if you're using CSS transitions, you can test the browser's ability to render these and, if the browser doesn't handle animations, provide a fallback or alternative.

Modernizr lets you write conditional CSS and JavaScript to tailor the experience of your web site according to the capabilities of the user's web browser. This is a useful technique for the whole of the CSS specification, but in this case it's handy specifically because you can test for support of new layout modules.

The library is quick to install and simple to use. When a page with Modernizr loads, a JavaScript object is created that contains the results of the tests, and CSS classes are added to the `<html>` element, allowing you to check via either script or CSS whether a specific feature is supported.

As I mentioned, you can conduct tests for feature support. That may leave you wondering what tests specifically can be run, and which features are supported by Modernizr. What makes the library so useful and popular is that it's almost a one-stop shop for browser functionality-support testing. Modernizr allows you to test for more than 40 next-generation features including `font-face`, `rgba`, CSS animations, gradients, canvas, HTML5 audio and video, local storage, and WebGL. And, most crucially, it can be used to test for the CSS3 layout modules discussed in this book!

The library doesn't force you to run tests for every single feature; a great strength of Modernizr is its modular nature. You only need to test the features you require, rather than having to conduct every individual feature test (see Figure 8-3).

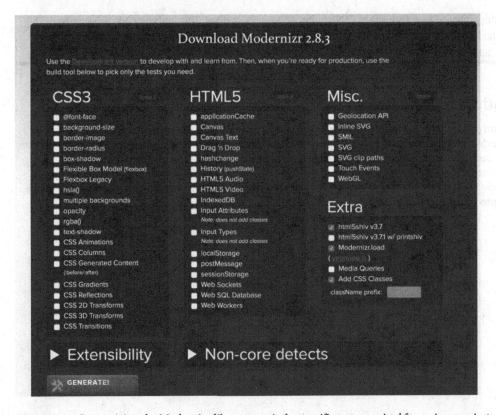

Figure 8-3. *Customizing the Modernizr library to suit the specific tests required for a given project*

THREE ALTERNATIVE METHODS TO TEST FEATURE SUPPORT IN BROWSERS

On the Server

If you're concerned about relying on JavaScript to identify browser features, you can use server-side sniffing instead. This approach uses the browser's `user agent` property to inject a browser-specific class into the `html` element before the page is sent to the browser. Note that this has the same potential problems as browser-sniffing of any kind: it doesn't scale well.

Conditional Comments

Another potential solution to addressing deficient browsers is to use conditional comments to selectively load stylesheets and scripts. This method is commonly used to target IE6 and IE7 and allows for loading according to version number as well as vendor, although support is limited to Internet Explorer.

@supports

One of the proposed new features of CSS3 is the `@supports` method. This lets you code a conditional test of the browser's ability to render a specific CSS property, and it works in a manner similar to `@media` queries. Ironically, the biggest issue with `@supports` is a lack of browser support.

Alternatives to Modernizr

It's important to highlight that Modernizr isn't the only solution available to polyfilling missing support in browsers. Indeed, Modernizr itself only really interrogates the browser to test for support for specific features and updates the DOM accordingly to signpost what is and is not available in terms of support.

As with any library on the Web, it pays to do a little research in your favorite search engine, because the landscape is changing rapidly (see Figure 8-4). One advantage of using Modernizr is that because it's so widely adopted, bug fixes tend to be released regularly.

Figure 8-4. *More than 20,000 results when searching for a polyfill for CSS Multi-columns Layout*

■ **Note** I can't stress enough the importance of checking the Web for the latest and greatest polyfill solutions at the time of authoring your page. The landscape is fluid enough that by the time you read this book, there could be many new solutions that improve on what's available today.

YepNope

YepNope hooks into the results of specific Modernizr tests and uses them to load resources into the browser (see Figure 8-5). This is incredibly useful: if you're able to split out your code into separate sections, the addition of YepNope allows you to conditionally load scripts and stylesheets.

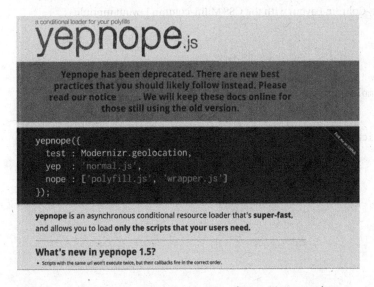

Figure 8-5. *The YepNope download page at* `http://yepnopejs.com`

Because it's only called into action after the Modernizr tests have run, you gain the major benefit of conditionally loading scripts and styles according to browser feature support and avoid having to load all your workaround options into every browser. Only those that need the polyfills get them. When combined with the prebuilt polyfill solutions described later in this chapter, Modernizr with YepNope almost offers a drag-and-drop solution to many compatibility issues you face when implementing CSS3 layout modules in production web sites.

Note that at the time of writing, YepNope is being discontinued because Modernizr has been updated to incorporate sufficient functionality to make the YepNope loader unnecessary. If you're using the most up-to-date version of Modernizr, you almost certainly no longer need YepNope, but I've mentioned it here in case you're stuck using older releases in a corporate environment.

▪ **Tip** Check `http://caniuse.com` to view a table showing the latest level of browser support for individual CSS layout modules.

Example Using Modernizr

Let's take a quick look at an example of a polyfill that uses Modernizr to provide CSS3-like support to older browsers that don't natively support the module you're using. This example styles a simple unordered list using the CSS3 Multi-column Layout module to spread the content of a list across a series of columns. In most modern browsers, this works without any need for either vendor prefixes or special workarounds. Check out `http://caniuse.com/#feat=multicolumn` for the latest on browser support. Note that Internet Explorer 8 and 9 don't offer any support for this module.

The Project

First, you generate an HTML document with some very basic styles to create a simple multicolumn layout. You can see the code for this in Listing 8-1 and the output in Safari in Figure 8-6.

Listing 8-1. Code to Achieve a Three-Column Layout with the CSS Multi-column Layout module

```
<!DOCTYPE HTML>
<html>
 <head>
  <meta http-equiv="Content-Type" content="text/html; charset=UTF-8">
   <title>Multicol Polyfill Example</title>
   <style>
    body {
     font-family: arial, helvetica, sans-serif;
     font-size: 62.5%;
     background: #fff;
     color:#333;
     }
    article {
     background: #eee;
     position: relative;
     padding: 20px;
     width: 920px;
     margin: auto;
}
```

```
    article h1 {
    font-size: 2em;
}
    article ul {
    columns: 3;
    }
    article ul li {
    list-style: none;
    font-size: 1.2em;
    padding: 5px;
}

  </style>
</head>
<body>
<article>
<h1>Things that I like</h1>
<ul>
  <li>Coffee</li>
  <li>Tea</li>
  <li>The Java Jive</li>
  <li>Lazy Sunday mornings</li>
  <li>A good book</li>
  <li>Nights at the movies</li>
  <li>The smell of baking bread</li>
  <li>Smiling</li>
  <li>Old-fashioned jazz and blues</li>
  <li>A freshly-made bed</li>
  <li>Hugs</li>
  </ul>
 </article>
</body>
</html>
```

Things that I like

Coffee	A good book	Old-fashioned jazz and blues
Tea	Nights at the movies	A freshly-made bed
The Java Jive	The smell of baking bread	Hugs
Lazy Sunday mornings	Smiling	

Figure 8-6. *Output of Listing 8-1 in Safari on a Mac*

As you can see, the code creates a basic three-column layout by adding the CSS code columns: 3 to the stylesheet, applying the rule to the ul element. This works in every browser in common use, with the exception of Internet Explorer 8 and Internet Explorer 9. You can't absolutely guarantee that users will be limited to the browsers in common use, however. To ensure that users of browsers that do not support CSS Multi-column Layout also see the list rendered into three columns, you can use Modernizr to test for support and, if no support is found, use a polyfill to render the columns.

The Polyfill

This is a very basic layout, so you don't need anything fancy or spectacular to work around lack of browser support. You can use a polyfill built specifically for the purpose of rendering content in multiple columns: Multicolumn-Polyfill, which you can find and download at https://github.com/hamsterbacke23/multicolumn-polyfill.

Before you can use the script, you need to ensure that Modernizr is installed and active on your page. Add a single line of code to the <head> section of the page to call in a CDN-hosted version of the Modernizr library, as shown in Listing 8-2.

Listing 8-2. Adding a CDN-Hosted Version of the Modernizr Library

```
<head>
 <meta http-equiv="Content-Type" content="text/html; charset=UTF-8">
 <title>Multicol Polyfill Example</title>
 <script src="jquery.js"></script>
 <script src="https://cdnjs.cloudflare.com/ajax/libs/modernizr/2.8.3/modernizr.min.js">
 </script>
 <style>
  body {
   font-family: arial, helvetica, sans-serif;
   font-size: 62.5%;
   background: #fff;
   color: #333;
  }
```

Now that you have both jQuery and the Modernizr library installed on the page, you can use a simple test in JavaScript to check whether the browser supports the CSS Multi-column Layout module. Add this to the code immediately before the closing </body> tag, as shown in Listing 8-3.

Listing 8-3. Test and Polyfill in Action

```
   <li>Hugs</li>
   </ul>
   </article>
   <script src="polyfill/multicolumn.js"></script>
   <script>
    if (!Modernizr.csscolumns) {
      $('article ul').multicolumn();
    }
   </script>
 </body>
</html>
```

The result of this additional code is that if the browser fails the Modernizr test for multicolumn support, the polyfill is loaded. The polyfill renders the content across columns using floated elements and hides the original container. It's as straightforward and simple as that.

This specific example addresses a very simple layout issue with a polyfill, but the same principle applies no matter how complicated your requirements become. Breaking down each element and polyfilling is a case of identifying features, testing for support, and then providing a fallback alternative for those layout elements. Note that support for specific browsers isn't guaranteed. It's down to the specific polyfill you choose, as illustrated by IE9 not rendering columns using the earlier example.

■ **Note**   Modernizr is undergoing a big new release at the time of writing. Rather than downloading or installing an entire library, you can copy and paste specific test code that's specific to the features you want to check against. Be sure to visit the Modernizr web site to get the latest version of the library.

Prebuilt Polyfills

Sometimes, an off-the-shelf polyfill solution won't work for your specific needs, in which case you may find yourself building your own script that provides functionality to substitute in place of the missing support. In most cases, however, simply using Modernizr, YepNope, and a prebuilt polyfill script is enough to get by. Also note that other options are available that don't use Modernizr.

To give you an idea of the range of existing polyfills that cover layout modules, following is a slightly curated list borrowed from the Modernizr blog (which has an extensive list of options). To see the full list, visit the link in the Note:

- *CSS Multi-column Layout*: Multicolumn polyfill by Cédric Savarese, `http:// alistapart.com/article/css3multicolumn`

- *CSS Flexible Box Layout*: Flexie by Richard Herrera, `http://flexiejs.com`

- *CSS Grid Layout*: Grid layout polyfill by François Remy, `https://github.com/ FremyCompany/css-grid-polyfill`

- *CSS Template Layout*: CSS Template Layout jQuery plug-in by Alexis Deveria, `https://code.google.com/p/css-template-layout/`

- *CSS Regions Layout*: Regions polyfill by François Remy, `https://github.com/ FremyCompany/css-regions-polyfill`

■ **Note**   For a full list of polyfills specific to each of the layout modules you've seen in this book, refer to the Modernizr blog post on the subject at `https://github.com/Modernizr/Modernizr/wiki/HTML5-Cross-Browser-Polyfills`.

Summary

Although it's easy to get carried away when new functionality becomes available, especially on the Web where standards are historically very slow to be implemented, it's important not to lose sight of the need to support older browsers, which can make up a substantial proportion of the users visiting your web sites. Polyfills offer a practical solution to providing support in many cases. Where this isn't practical or possible, for technical or resource reasons, taking a progressive enhancement approach can offer a useful alternative that ensures your content is accessible and user-friendly.

As browser support improves and users update their systems to utilize the latest software, polyfills should become less prevalent. But for the time being, they're worth using any time you want to use one of the layout modules discussed in this book and can't control the audience's operating system and device profiles.

Don't forget to regularly check for new and improved polyfills via your favorite search engine. Talented web developers the world over are constantly constructing solutions to the issue of modules not yet being implemented in common browsers.

CHAPTER 9

■■■

Speeding Up Workflow: CSS Libraries and Frameworks

Working in web design involves a lot of repetition: although every page is unique, much of the underlying code relies on the same core principles and building blocks. The layout modules that CSS3 introduces offer a tidy solution for lots of different layout paradigms, but they can be unnecessarily complex when you're crafting essentially the same layout over and over. How do you reduce the time and complexity overhead when working with core building blocks? By using CSS libraries and frameworks, you can simplify the layout process, abstracting some of the complications and providing a consistent, rapid development platform.

You are most likely familiar with many such frameworks and libraries; they're not new or limited to CSS3 layout modules. Some of the Web's most popular web sites are built on top of frameworks made open source by the developer teams behind Twitter, Microsoft, Apple, and Facebook. Examples include the likes of Bootstrap, which provides a simple solution to creating many elements of a layout in a responsive fashion that works well for almost every possible device. These frameworks all tend to remove the direct connection with the underpinning CSS code, making development a case of applying the appropriate structure and CSS classes to individual elements in the page structure.

Many libraries and frameworks deal with much more than just layout. Much of the functionality baked in also allows you to craft widgets and buttons and style copy and headlines in a consistent manner. This can have benefits, but if you only wanted to be able to design using a predefined set of styles, you wouldn't have this book in your hands! This chapter introduces you to some of the best CSS3 layout libraries and frameworks, with a specific focus on keeping the job of styling in your control. Inevitably you'll find one that you prefer, and you'll stick with that. It's worth regularly checking the Web to see what new frameworks have been developed by the online community (see, for example, Figure 9-1), because the environment is so fluid that things can change very quickly.

■ **Tip** Once you've found a library that you like, spending time getting to know its nuances can pay big rewards later. But don't ever sit back and accept that you've found the pinnacle of the library/framework options. It pays to shop around!

© Sam Hampton-Smith 2016
S. Hampton-Smith, *Pro CSS3 Layout Techniques*, DOI 10.1007/978-1-4302-6503-0_9

CSS Frameworks & UI Kits

Kindling – A responsive grid system with minimal styling and markup.

Webplate – A fully featured frontend framework.

Figure 9-1. *There are many web sites dedicated to showcasing CSS3 libraries and frameworks, such as SpeckyBoy (http://speckyboy.com/2014/06/02/css-libraries-frameworks-tools/)*

Don't Start from Scratch

Libraries and frameworks come in a variety of forms. Some are full-on web site development tools that act as a scaffold for page layouts, design implementation, and content styling. Others take a more structural approach, providing building blocks and getting out the way of the business of aesthetically treating the elements on the page.

Both approaches have their plusses and minuses, but they share a common goal: speeding up the development of pages and making it easier to achieve consistency in your code. You don't need to start from scratch with each new page that you design: instead, by calling on a suitable library, you can use the work of others to reduce repeated effort.

Developers and designers tend to find a tool they like and stick with it. This can yield benefits when you're using a particular library or framework, because as you become more comfortable and familiar with the methodology of a specific code base, you can take best advantage of what it offers. Being loyal to one tool can have its downsides, too, not least because without seeing what else is available, you may miss out on enhanced functionality and capabilities offered elsewhere. So I encourage you to try your finger in many different library and framework pies and to keep sampling on an ongoing basis.

An argument that is often leveled against the use of other developers' code is that you may become dependent on that vendor's willingness and ability to squash bugs and provide updates and revisions. There's also the time investment required to learn the nuances of each specific codebase. I would like to convince you that a bit of investment up front can bring great benefits in time (and money) down the line.

Another issue worth talking about, and one that libraries and frameworks tend to alleviate without you having to worry much about it, is cross-browser operability. Although some of the worst CSS-implementation differences are (fortunately) now in the past, there continue to be different interpretations of how individual modules from the specification should be integrated. This is especially true with emerging modules such as those you've seen in this book. By using a library, an example of which you can see in

Figure 9-2, you can eliminate much of the uncertainty in providing vendor-prefixed versions of selectors. This means you have more time to spend on the overall layout, rather than wasting time figuring out why a particular browser isn't implementing your design the same way every other browser does.

Figure 9-2. *The YAML webpage, found at* `http://www.yaml.de`

Again, countering this benefit is the fact that libraries can sometimes be bloated and cumbersome, which means they may impact the performance of your web site. Additional code to support every device under the Sun, when you're only interested in targeting your company's corporate devices, may outweigh some of the positives of using a library.

There's No Right Answer for Libraries and Frameworks

As you can see, there's are arguments in favor of and against using CSS libraries and frameworks. The question of whether it's appropriate for your specific project can only be answered by your own analysis and, often, a judgment call on your part.

Recognizing that there are occasions when it's beneficial to use them, however, the rest of this chapter is dedicated to examining a few options that are available at the time of writing. Toward the end of the chapter, you also revisit a project completed in Chapter 5 and see how it might be interpreted and implemented differently if you were using a library instead of raw CSS code.

■ **Note** Some libraries and frameworks use a hybrid approach of employing CSS3 layout modules and non-CSS3 layout tricks. Unless you're a purist, this can offer a good, robust solution to the problem of achieving a specific layout.

The Best CSS Frameworks and Libraries

Given that you're working in a very fluid time for CSS3 layout modules, this section's heading is bold, but I've picked out some of the best CSS frameworks and libraries currently available. How do I know they're the best? I've conducted an entirely unscientific study of search-engine results to determine popular opinion. I'll keep saying this: it's imperative that you check out what the online community has to say when you embark on a search for a library.

As discussed earlier, two basic types of libraries and frameworks are available. The difference is a little like that between a basic motel room and a five-star hotel room. Sometimes you want nothing more than four walls and a bed, with the ability to cook your own food and use your room as you see fit; other times, you want the luxury of letting someone else worry about the details, and to have everything brought to you on a silver platter!

At its most basic level, a CSS3 layout library only provides the hooks to allow you to create a grid layout, render a flexbox, or call on a multicolumn layout, without having to do anything more than apply the appropriate classnames to a series of <div>s, <section>s, or <article>s. These are akin to a basic motel room. They do one thing, and that's it. The rest is up to you! At the other end are solutions that do all the layout and that also offer widgets, styles, and skins that can essentially provide every facility you might need to achieve a page design and layout, including all the aesthetics.

I err on the side of the motel room. But don't let that stop you from pursuing the full-service option if it suits your needs more effectively for a particular project.

Flexbox Grid

The Flexbox Grid system is a straightforward library designed to allow you to use classes on elements to assign different Flexbox attributes to the layout without having to dig into CSS directly (see Figure 9-3). Created by Kristopher Joseph, it's an extremely lightweight solution, barely abstracting the source CSS3 Flexbox code; but because of this, it is also really easy to learn how to use. Later in this chapter, you use this library to re-create the original Flexbox project.

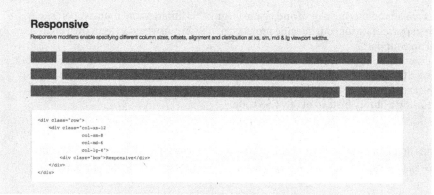

Figure 9-3. Flexbox Grid, found at http://flexboxgrid.com

ptb/flexgrid

This framework is also based on the Flexbox module, but rather than offer the bare bones, it attempts to re-create the same layout paradigm that Bootstrap uses (see Figure 9-4). The resulting grid layout is far more rigid than with other options, but if you're already familiar with the Bootstrap 12-column grid, you'll immediately feel right at home.

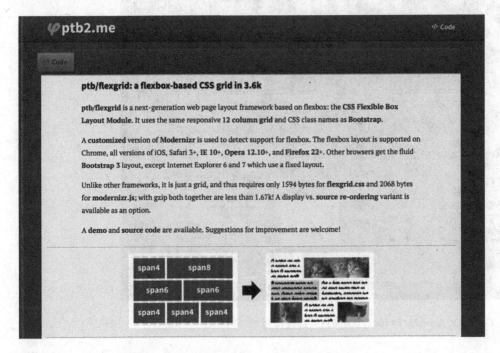

Figure 9-4. *ptb/flexbox, found at* `http://ptb2.me/flexgrid/`

ptb/flexgrid is designed solely for the purpose of laying out content in a grid system—there's no fancy user-control styling or additional widgets. The result is that the entire framework occupies less than 2 KB, excluding the Modernizr library, which is required to ensure that the layout works across all browsers.

Compass

Compass differs from the other libraries and frameworks highlighted in this section in that it doesn't simply use a single CSS3 layout module, but rather provides a solution to make it easier to use any and all of the tools available in CSS3, and CSS in general (see Figure 9-5). The premise is simple: reduce the amount of code clutter associated with crafting a specific design, and provide easy access to reusable design patterns that are popular across the Web. This means you can use the framework to rapidly prototype and deploy a layout using building blocks you're familiar with. There are also a host of extensions available that cover everything from typographic control to sprite generation.

Figure 9-5. Compass, found at http://compass-style.org

CSS Regions Polyfill

Although Francois Remy's CSS Regions Polyfill isn't technically a framework, I've included it here because it offers a really useful solution for using the CSS Regions Layout specification immediately (see Figure 9-6). The particular benefit of using Francois' JavaScript library is that it allows you to implement regions without browser vendor prefixes, enabling you to write code today that still needs direct access and understanding of the CSS Regions Layout module but that is future-proofed while remaining accessible to older browsers, thanks to JavaScript.

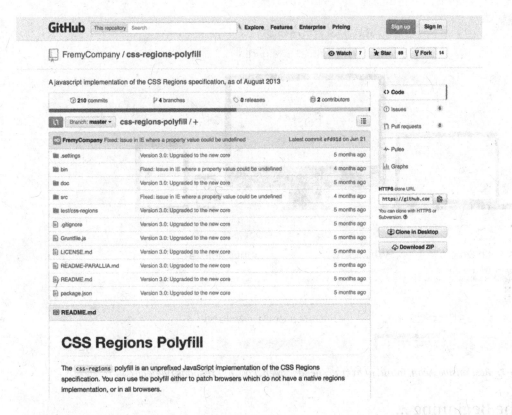

Figure 9-6. CSS Regions Polyfill, found at https://github.com/FremyCompany/css-regions-polyfill

Because the library uses the original specification, you don't need to know anything other than what's covered in this book. This won't simplify your code, but it removes a headache in providing cross-browser support and fallback.

Responsive Aeon

This grid-based library uses an approach similar to some of the other libraries highlighted here, but the layout engineering is completely abstracted, so it's not immediately obvious which modules are being used to create the layout (see Figure 9-7). In fact, the latest update uses a lot of CSS2.1 to produce the layout, while using an approach similar to that of CSS3 Grid Layout. Remember that when you're using a CSS layout, you're calling on a combination of decades of work; so if you need something a little more stable than the fluid "in-development" CSS3 modules, this may be a good stepping stone toward a fully CSS3 solution. The code is very simple, so it's also ripe for customization to form the basis of a library you can reuse in future projects.

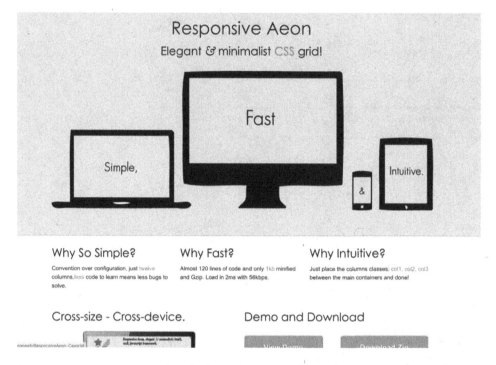

Figure 9-7. *Responsive Aeon, found at* `http://newaeonweb.com.br/responsiveaeon/`

Just the Beginning ...

Keep in mind that the libraries and frameworks highlighted in this chapter are just the beginning of the options available on the Web. To speed up your workflow, it's crucial that you invest time early on examining and exploring the options available to you.

■ **Note**　Here I am, saying again that I can't stress enough the importance of checking the Web for the latest and greatest libraries and frameworks available when you author your page. By the time you read this book, there will almost certainly be a host of options that add to the mix available at the time of writing.

Speeding Up Your Workflow: An Example

Now that you've seen a few of the options currently available for speeding up page development using CSS libraries and frameworks, let's dig into one in more detail and see what it might look like to use one of these libraries. For the purposes of this exploration, let's return to an example projects you saw earlier in the book. This is useful because it allows you to see how code crafted earlier can be simplified through the use of a framework.

A Real-World Example

If you haven't already checked out Chapter 5, take a quick look now to familiarize yourself with CSS Flexbox and how it works to fill space. This example re-creates the project featured in that chapter; but instead of using raw CSS Flexbox code, it takes advantage of the Flexbox Grid library and shows the effect the library has on the code.

Let's recall the layout you're seeking to create. Figure 9-8 shows the mockup from Chapter 5; this example uses the exact same elements to craft another version of this project, but it should be significantly easier once you're familiar with the Flexbox Grid library.

Figure 9-8. *The project to be re-created from Chapter 5 using a library instead of raw CSS flexbox code*

If you've been paying attention, you realize that Flexbox was used to create the layout in Figure 9-9. For the purpose of providing a fair comparison, you'll use the same module to render the layout of the library-powered layout. This means calling on the Flexbox Grid library highlighted earlier in this chapter. I'm not endorsing that particular library; but as you'll see, it does provide an effective and functional solution to crafting the layout. Just as in the previous layout attempt, let's focus exclusively on three sections of the page: the navigation bar, jumbotron area, and benefit statements.

The HTML Markup

Let's begin by looking at the HTML markup used in Chapter 5, shown in Listing 9-1. The code for this page is straightforward and follows a pattern similar to layouts used in the past when using floats to arrange design elements.

Listing 9-1. HTML Code for Three Parts of the Page Suited to Flexbox Layout

```html
<!—The navigation section -->
<nav>
 <ul>
  <li><a href="#">Home</a></li>
  <li><a href="#">Locations</a></li>
  <li><a href="#">Financing</a></li>
  <li><a href="#">Special Offers</a></li>
  <li><a href="#">About us</a></li>
  <li><a href="#">Contact Us</a></li>
  <li class="searchform"><form><input type="text" value="search" /></form></li>
 </ul>
</nav>

<!—The big icons/jumbotron section -->
<section id="jumbotron">
 <article>
  <h2>Free Advice</h2>
  <p>All our impartial advice is offered completely free of charge</p>
  <img src="images/bigicon-freeadvice.png" />
 </article>
 <article>
  <h2>Discounted Removals</h2>
  <p>Once you've found your dream…
...</article>
</section>

<!—The badge benefits section -->
<section id="benefits">
  <article>
   <h1> Looking for a beautiful new home that won't break the bank?</h1>
   <p> Nulla vitae elit libero, a pharetra augue. Nulla vitae elit libero, a pharetra augue.
   Cras mattis consectetur purus sit amet fermentum.</p>
  </article>
  <article class="badge">
   <div>
    <h3>Quality without compromise</h3>
    <p>We have homes that suit every budget without compromising on quality</p>
   </div>
   <img src="images/badge-quality.png" />
  </article>
  <article class="badge">...
  ...</article>
</section>
```

Using the Library

Different libraries have different solutions for implementation. This example uses the Flexbox Grid library, so you download the library and follow the instructions for inserting it into my page. This is as simple as creating a <link> in the <head> section, as shown in Listing 9-2.

Listing 9-2. Installing the Library by Copying Files into the Web Site Folders and Using a <link> Statement

```
<head>
  ...
  <link rel="stylesheet" href="css/flexboxgrid.min.css" type="text/css">
  ...
</head>
```

■ **Tip** Recall that as new CSS3 modules are implemented by browser vendors, they tend to start with vendor-specific prefixes in their implementation. Libraries and frameworks remove the need for you to concern yourself with these nuances.

The Navigation

The first section of the page you need to deal with is the navigation that runs across the top of the design. This, as you see if you refer back to Chapter 5, is pretty simple using Flexbox directly. Listing 9-3 repeats the CSS code used in Chapter 5, to illustrate just how simple! Using the Flexbox Grid library is equally straightforward, as shown in Listing 9-4.

Listing 9-3. Native Flexbox CSS Code to Create the Navigation Layout

```
/* The navigation section */
nav > ul {
  display: flex;
  flex-flow: row wrap;
}
nav > ul > .searchform {
  margin-left: auto;
}
```

Listing 9-4. Using the Flexbox Grid Library and Altering the HTML Code to Apply Specific Classes to Elements

```
<!—The navigation section -->
<nav>
  <ul class="row start-xs">
    <li class="col-xs"><a href="#">Home</a></li>
    <li class="col-xs"><a href="#">Locations</a></li>
    <li class="col-xs"><a href="#">Financing</a></li>
    <li class="col-xs"><a href="#">Special Offers</a></li>
    <li class="col-xs"><a href="#">About us</a></li>
    <li class="col-xs"><a href="#">Contact Us</a></li>
```

```
<li class="col-xs-offset-2 col-xs searchform"><form><input type="text" value="search" />
</form></li>
 </ul>
</nav>
```

As you can see, the primary difference between the two approaches is that when you handle the implementation by writing CSS Flexbox code directly, you use CSS to create the layout. In the case of the Flexbox Grid library, you instead apply class names to the HTML. In this example, the difference is trivial; but as things get more complex, the second approach is more agile if you wish to make changes to the number of items that appear in the layout. Figure 9-9 shows the navigation output in Chrome after implementing the Flexbox Grid library.

Figure 9-9. *If you're eagle-eyed, you'll notice that this is practically the same as the render in Chapter 5 following the native CSS attempt. The primary difference is that this version aligns to a grid*

The Jumbotron

Using straight CSS, the jumbotron was pretty straightforward to craft. Recall the following about the design mockup that can help when turning this into a functioning layout:

- Each <article> is evenly sized.

- The content of each element in the jumbotron is aligned centrally on both axes.

- The image renders before the text but appears after the text in the markup.

Check back to the HTML code, and notice that the last point requires you to reorder the content during presentation. Flexbox makes this straightforward, and so does the Flexbox Grid library. Again, everything is handled by applying specific classes to the elements in the markup. The code using the library is shown in Listing 9-5.

Listing 9-5. Flexbox Grid Classes Applied to the HTML Markup, Assigning Layout Attributes to the Elements on the Page

```
<!—The big icons/jumbotron section -->
<section id="jumbotron" class="row">
 <article class="col-lg-4 col-xs-12">
  <div class="marginbox row">
   <h2 class="col-xs-12">Free Advice</h2>
   <p class="col-xs-12">All our impartial advice is offered completely free of charge</p>
   <div class="col-xs-12 first-xs"><img src="images/bigicon-freeadvice.png" width="52"
   height="41" /></div>
  </div>
 </article>
 <article class="col-lg-4 col-xs-12">
  <div class="marginbox row">
```

```
 <h2 class="col-xs-12">Discounted Removals</h2>
 <p class="col-xs-12">Once you've found your dream home we can help get you moved in</p>
 <div class="col-xs-12 first-xs"><img src="images/bigicon-removals.png" width="50"
 height="41" /></div>
 </div>
</article>
<article class="col-lg-4 col-xs-12">
 <div class="marginbox row">
 <h2 class="col-xs-12">Buying Incentives</h2>
 <p class="col-xs-12">Many of our homes offer additional benefits such as rebates</p>
 <div class="col-xs-12 first-xs"><img src="images/bigicon-incentives.png" width="24"
 height="41" /></div>
 </div>
</article>
<article class="col-lg-4 col-xs-12">
 <div class="marginbox row">
 <h2 class="col-xs-12">Locations nationwide</h2>
 <p class="col-xs-12">We have agents and properties across all 50 States</p>
 <div class="col-xs-12 first-xs"><img src="images/bigicon-locations.png" width="41"
 height="41" /></div>
 </div>
</article>
<article class="col-lg-4 col-xs-12">
 <div class="marginbox row">
 <h2 class="col-xs-12">Highest Quality Homes</h2>
 <p class="col-xs-12">Every single home we offer is guaranteed for quality</p>
 <div class="col-xs-12 first-xs"><img src="images/bigicon-quality.png" width="51"
 height="41" /></div>
 </div>
</article>
<article class="col-lg-4 col-xs-12">
 <div class="marginbox row">
 <h2 class="col-xs-12">No obligation</h2>
 <p class="col-xs-12">You can withdraw from the process at any time without penalty</p>
 <div class="col-xs-12 first-xs"><img src="images/bigicon-noobligation.png" width="45"
 height="41" /></div>
 </div>
</article>
</section>
```

Changing the HTML also means the original CSS is no longer relevant. You can remove all the Flexbox code, as shown in Listing 9-6, leaving the classes assigned in Listing 9-5.

Listing 9-6. Removing the Flexbox Code from the CSS Used in Chapter 5, and Thus Simplifying the Code

```
/* The jumbotron section */
#jumbotron {
 background: #38CEB1;
 max-width:    960px;
 min-height:   380px;
```

```css
 justify-content: center;
 padding-left: 1px;
}
#jumbotron article {
 /* Vertical align */
 justify-content: center;
 text-align: center;
}
.marginbox {
 /* Vertical align */
 justify-content: center;
 text-align: center;
 min-height: 190px;
 background: #EAEAEA;
 margin: 0 1px 1px 0;
}

#jumbotron article .marginbox * {
 align-self: center;
}

#jumbotron article .marginbox:hover {
 background: #efefef;
}
```

The result, rendered in Safari, is shown in Figure 9-10. Note that this alternative approach requires that you add an additional `<div>` element around the content of each article. This is to allow for the margin between articles, which would otherwise cause only two articles to render per row. I've also set this additional `<div>` to work as a nested Flexbox grid row, ensuring that the three elements flex as the design calls for. Every other aspect of the rendering is identical.

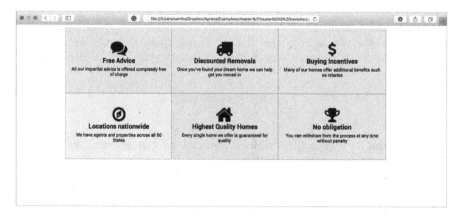

Figure 9-10. *The output from Listing 9-6 is identical to the original version created in Chapter 5*

In case you were wondering what happens when the browser window is narrower than 960px, the benefits of Flexbox continue to apply here. When the window gets a little narrower, the content repaginates. This is thanks to the ability to assign multiple classes to each element. In this case, I assigned an extra-small screen to show each `<article>` at 12-column width (which fills the entire row), meaning only one `<article>` is rendered per row.

The Benefits Area

The remaining section of the page originally rendered using Flexbox was the benefits section at the bottom. This, you may recall, was the most complicated of the three parts to craft.

The benefits section is more complicated because the column on the left is double the height of the sections on the right. In order to handle this, the HTML nests elements. You can see the required code when implementing the Flexbox Grid library in Listing 9-7. Again, some extra CSS code is required in addition to the layout hooks handled by the library, as shown in Listing 9-8. The resulting amount of code is broadly similar to the original version created in Chapter 5, but layout control has been migrated to the use of classes on the HTML elements rather than purely in CSS. This means changing the layout by introducing additional elements can be controlled directly from the HTML.

Listing 9-7. Required HTML Alterations

```
<!—The badge benefits section -->
<section id="benefits" class="row">
 <article class="col-lg-4">
  <h1>Looking for a beautiful new home that won't break the bank?</h1>
  <p>Nulla vitae elit libero, a pharetra augue. Nulla vitae elit libero, a pharetra augue.
  Cras mattis consectetur purus sit amet fermentum.</p>
  <p>Curabitur blandit tempus porttitor. Aenean eu leo quam.
 </article>
 <div class="col-lg-8 row">
  <article class="badge col-lg-6 row">
   <div class="col-lg-9 row">
    <h3 class="col-lg-12">Quality without compromise</h3>
    <p class="col-lg-12">We have homes that suit every budget without compromising on
    quality</p>
   </div>
   <div class="col-lg-3 first-xs"><img src="images/badge-quality.png" width="38"
   height="38" /></div>
  </article>
  <article class="badge col-lg-6 row">
   <div class="col-lg-9 row">
    <h3 class="col-lg-12">Trade-up facilities</h3>
    <p class="col-lg-12">If you have a home to sell, we can help market it, and arrange
    bridging finance</p>
   </div>
   <div class="col-lg-3 first-xs"><img src="images/badge-tradeup.png" width="38"
   height="38" /></div>
  </article>
  <article class="badge col-lg-6 row">
   <div class="col-lg-9 row">
    <h3 class="col-lg-12">Wonderful locations</h3>
```

```html
      <p class="col-lg-12">Don't settle for a nice home in a bad location. All our locations
      are carefully chosen</p>
      </div>
      <div class="col-lg-3 first-xs"><img src="images/badge-locations.png" width="38"
      height="38" /></div>
    </article>
    <article class="badge col-lg-6 row">
      <div class="col-lg-9 row">
        <h3 class="col-lg-12">Value-added service</h3>
        <p class="col-lg-12">We offer a range of packages that can add value to your home-buying
        experience, </p>
      </div>
      <div class="col-lg-3 first-xs"><img src="images/badge-valueadd.png" width="38"
      height="38" /></div>
    </article>
  </div>
</section>
```

Listing 9-8. CSS to Size Elements on the Page

```css
/* The badge benefits section */
#benefits {
 width:    960px;
 max-width: 960px;
 margin-top: 50px;
 height: 260px;
}
#benefits article.badge img {
 margin:  0.5em 0;
 margin-right: 10px;
}
#benefits article h1 {
 font-size:  2em;
 padding-right: 1em;
 font-weight:  normal;
 margin-bottom:  0.5em;
}
#benefits article h3 {
 font-size:  1.6em;
 font-weight:  normal;
 margin:  0;
 padding-left: 0;
 text-align:   left;
}
#benefits article p {
 text-align:   left;
 padding:  0;
 font-size:  1.2em;
 margin-bottom:  1em;
}
```

The output from this implementation is shown in Figure 9-11. Notice that once again the result is nearly identical to the original version from Chapter 5. This is to be expected, because fundamentally the code is the same between the two implementations; the difference is in how you assign the attributes to the markup. Which methodology you prefer is up to you, but it can be useful to have prebuilt libraries that create the layout along common design patterns without the need to create your own solution each time.

Figure 9-11. *The output in Safari*

■ **Note**   Just to reiterate, some additional non-Flexbox CSS code is required to define the color, border, and typographic styles shown in this example. I've intentionally trimmed the code snippets to only show the relevant CSS code for layout.

Summary

This chapter looked at ways you can use CSS libraries and frameworks to speed up page development. Although it's tempting to reinvent the wheel each time you embark on a page layout, fundamentally the same core elements underpin almost every page you'll ever design. By recognizing this fact and using a library to hasten layout, you can focus on getting the details of the design right.

Naturally, there will be times when a library or framework won't work for your project, so don't be scared to admit that you need to roll your own solution from time to time. It's much better to recognize this early in the development process, rather than have a horrible lightbulb moment after you've invested hours and hours shoehorning a design into a framework. For this reason, a little time invested up front to investigate all the options and choose the one that's best suited to your specific project is well spent—even if it results in you not using a library!

■ ■ ■

What the Future Holds for CSS Layout

Congratulations! You've reached the end of this book on the current layout options offered as part of CSS3. But don't think this is the end of the story!

Along the way to this chapter, you've delved into CSS Flexbox, CSS Multi-column Layout, CSS Regions Layout, and CSS Grid Layout, and you even took a quick look back what the past offered in terms of alternatives. It's my hope that you've also picked up some ideas for how to polyfill missing functionality and use the principles of progressive enhancement to offer new and improved layouts for the increasing majority of users with the latest browsers while not excluding those stuck on older browsers.

It's All Still Being Developed

CSS3 is very much in active development, as you've seen by the transient nature of some of the modules discussed in this book. And it's not just the modules I've talked about that are still undergoing development—more goodies are in the works that may bring entirely new paradigms to the layout you use on a daily basis.

During the process of writing and researching this book, there have been numerous whispers about exciting new developments going on in the likes of Adobe, Microsoft, Apple, and Mozilla. The years in the 2000s that saw stagnation in the development of CSS are firmly at an end; and as more and more consumers embrace new technologies and demand more from their online experiences, the companies responsible for delivering the framework to support those experiences are listening and reacting!

One example is Adobe. Adobe, famous for its desktop-publishing and creative tools, is intent on embracing the digital future—and what better platform than the open Web? In addition to cosponsoring many of the modules you've already seen, numerous others are being discussed in development rooms at the software giant.

Upcoming Modules and Ideas

I hope you've picked up on the fact that we're in a really exciting phase of development in CSS. The language is developing rapidly, and ideas are being thrown around without much fear. This means there is a lot of engagement, and designers and technicians are buying into the idea of further development. Let's have a quick look at a pair of future modules that may make the cut.

© Sam Hampton-Smith 2016
S. Hampton-Smith, *Pro CSS3 Layout Techniques*, DOI 10.1007/978-1-4302-6503-0_10

CSS Exclusions

CSS Exclusions has developed beyond a behind-closed-doors discussion and is now in development via the W3C. It's currently in Working Draft form, cosponsored by Adobe and Microsoft; it builds on the idea of floating elements introduced in CSS2.1.

Similar in some ways to CSS Regions Layout, CSS Exclusions describe the way content can flow around elements, effectively adding another layout formatting tool to the designer's arsenal (see Figure 10-1). It's important to note that the specification is still at its earliest stages, so you won't be able to reliably use it in the very near future, but you can find out more at www.w3.org/TR/css3-exclusions/, where the current specification is available. Not much implementation is available at the time of writing, but this is potentially a small but significant improvement to the way you can control content in a more magazine-style manner.

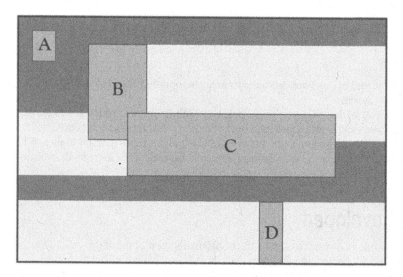

Figure 10-1. *The effect of CSS Exclusions on content, determining how wrapping should occur*

CSS Shapes

Although not exclusively about layout, CSS Shapes is another example of an upcoming specification; you can find out more at www.w3.org/TR/css-shapes/. Again, it builds on the idea of achieving a more magazine-like layout on the Web; in this case, it determines non-box-shaped boxes for content. This is a pretty big thing, because until now you've had to use smoke and mirrors to give the impression of dealing with something other than box-shaped content areas.

Again, this module is being co-sponsored by Adobe and Microsoft and is still in active development. Keep an eye on the web site to get the latest information about when you may be able to use this in earnest (without the current crop of script-based polyfills!). Figure 10-2 gives you an idea how significant this could be for formatting copy around images (or other content) on the Web.

Figure 10-2. A CSS shape acting based on the alpha channel of an image, wrapping content automatically around the image subject

And there's more …

The ideas being explored aren't limited to these two modules. Check out the CSS Working Group web site for more, including a Presentations Level module that determines styling according to content level—useful for PowerPoint-style presentations—and upgrades to the way paged media is dealt with on the Web. There's a lot more than I've had space to cover here, so it's well worth browsing to see what might be in the next edition of this book!

■ **Caution**   Things change over time! Don't forget to check back regularly with the authority on all things CSS3—the W3C—for revisions and enhancements to the specifications outlined in this book. There have been numerous developments over the time it's taken to write this book, and there will doubtless be many more before the complete set of modules are at release candidate stage. But then, that's part of the fun of working on the Web, isn't it?

Summary

This chapter has looked at how far we've come and the current state of affairs for CSS3 layout. I also took a sneaky glimpse at the future and what exciting new modules may be developed in the coming years. It's a fantastic time to be involved in web design; and with the improvements being made to the languages and technologies that power the Web and to the browsers that allow users to view and enjoy it, the future can only be bright for us as web designers. Go forth, and lay out!

Index

S. Hampton-Smith, *Pro CSS3 Layout Techniques*, DOI 10.1007/978-1-4302-6503-0

H, I, J, K

L

M, N, O

P, Q

R, S, T, U, V, W, X, Y

Z

Printed in the United States
By Bookmasters